Computer Electronics

IN THE SAME SERIES

BASIC
Computer Electronics
Computer Programming Languages in Practice
Systems Analysis
Word Processing for the Professions

Computer Electronics

Made Simple Computerbooks

J. F. B. Bourdillon, BSc(Eng), ACGI, AMIEE

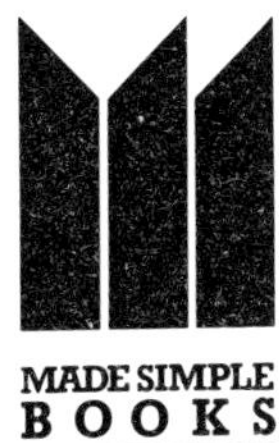

HEINEMANN : London

Printed and bound in Great Britain
by Richard Clay Ltd, Bungay
for the publishers William Heinemann Ltd,
10 Upper Grosvenor Street, London W1X 9PA

This book is dedicated to my parents, without whose considerable love and help this book would not have been written.

British Library Cataloguing in Publication Data
Bourdillon, J. F. B.
Computer electronics. — (Made simple computerbooks)
1 Microcomputers
I. Title II. Series
001.64'04 QA76.5

ISBN 0 434 98405 1

Contents

3 Making Your Own Circuits 18

4 More Complex Devices 33

5 Analog Components 52

6 Data Books and How to Use Them 64

14 The Project Life Cycle 169

Appendices 178

Index 188

CHAPTER RESUMÉ

Chapter 1 This chapter introduces the reader to the idea of hardware design. It covers binary and hexadecimal, Boolean Algebra and truth tables. An example of Boolean Algebra is given with respect to a voting problem.

Chapter 2 This chapter explains the basic building blocks of hardware (NAND, NOR, AND, OR, NOT, XOR). This example from Chapter 1 is put into logic using these gates.

Chapter 3 This chapter explains what tools and equipment are required by a hardware engineer. Photographs are used to enhance the explanations. Sources for tools and components are given, along with addresses. A brief explanation of how to solder is given. The example from Chapters 1 and 2 is built using 74LS series TTL. Wirewrapping is also explained.

Chapter 4 Sequential logic is covered in this chapter (J-K flip flop, 'D' flip flop, shift registers and counters). At each stage, practical exercises, using breadboards and veroboards, are included to give the reader confidence that he/she is learning. This chapter also explains some important practical design rules.

Chapter 5 This chapter explains transistors, resistors, capacitors, diodes, crystals, power supplies, etc. The explanations are biased towards the way in which the components are used in digital design (for instance in the design of a clock circuit).

Chapter 6 This chapter gently introduces the reader to data sheets and data books. It talks about the different types of TTL (LS, S, AS, etc.) and goes through all of the categories that are found in data sheets, explaining what information is useful and what can be ignored for difficult applications.

Chapter 7 This chapter introduces timing diagrams and explains why they are so useful. Examples of circuits and associated timing are given to aid comprehension.

Chapter 8 This chapter covers full adders, carry generators, ALUs and number processors. Practical exercises are given for the breadboard to allow the reader to see how the ICs work.

Chapter 9 This chapter explains how a microprocessor works. It centres around the Z80 and introduces assembly language programming. After reading this chapter, the reader should be confident enough to use a microprocessor.

Chapter 10 This chapter deals with the various types of PROMs, static RAMs, dynamic RAMs, floppy disks, hard disks, etc. The explanations are such that the reader could design using these devices.

Chapter 11 This chapter gives brief explanations of the microprocessor support devices made by Intel, Motorola and Zilog. Possible applications are discussed. The information given is not sufficient to design using these devices, but the reader is advised to buy the relevant data books.

Chapter 12 This chapter covers some TTL devices, widely used in design, that have not yet been discussed. The rationale behind this chapter is to increase the design repertoire of the reader.

Chapter 13 This chapter introduces bit slice logic and describes some AMD bit slice products. It also introduces custom IC design — gate arrays (semi custom) and full custom ICs.

Chapter 14 This chapter describes how a project operates and explains how the CAD process works and how PCBs are manufactured.

Note: Throughout the book, design rules are discussed as they crop up as are practical considerations, such as capacitors for decoupling.

Preface

This book has been written with three distinct purposes in mind:

1. It may be used by people who are interested in learning how to design using digital electronics. These people may or may not have any knowledge of electronics or computers.

2. It may be used by people new to design work coming from school or university. These people will have a reasonable theoretical knowledge in some fields, but will not necessarily have practical knowledge.

3. It may be used by people who are doing design work as a reference book.

This book will take the reader from the basics of hardware design to the intricacies of designing a microcomputer system. The book covers both the theoretical and practical considerations involved in hardware design.

Acknowledgements

Neil for checking the book at all of its stages and for invaluable suggestions. Tracy and David. Neil and Linda. CJ for the use of his uP. Bad and Sal for writing books first, thus proving that our family is not illiterate, and all other friends who have given advice.

Appendix D was taken mainly from *The TTL Data Book* (Vol. 1 Section 3), Texas Instruments Ltd, Manton Lane, Bedford MK41 7PA.

Figure 13.1 was taken from p. 5–5 of *Bipolar Microprocessor Logic and Interface Data Book* (1983), Advanced Micro Devices, AMD House, Goldsworth Road, Woking, Surrey, GU21 1JT.

Figures 9.4–9.10 were taken from *The Zilog Data Book* (1978), Zilog, Nicholson House, Maidenhead, Berkshire, SL6 1LD.

1
Fundamentals of Hardware Design

1.1 WHAT IS HARDWARE DESIGN?

Hardware design is concerned with building electrical circuits which perform various functions. These circuits range from computers to video tape recorders.

The way these circuits are made is to connect other, more simple, circuits together. The way these simple circuits are made is irrelevant to the hardware designer—all that is important is the function of the circuit (i.e. what happens at the output(s) when the input(s) are changed). In this sense, the circuit is merely a black box with instructions explaining its use.

Hence hardware design consists of connecting black boxes together in a particular way to perform some function. These black boxes may be anything from resistors, transistors, etc. at the small end, to an IBM 370 computer at the large end. The key to hardware design is threefold:

1. You need to know the exact function of your black box.
2. You need to know the rules for interconnecting it to other black boxes.
3. You need to work out exactly what the design must do (Functional Requirements).

These rules apply to many other fields than just hardware design. For instance, if you wanted to light 8 torchbulbs for $2\frac{1}{2}$ hours, then you might go about it in the following manner:

Black box 1: Torchbulb.
Black box 2: Battery.

Function of each black box

The torchbulb will light if there is 3V between its inputs.
The battery will produce 3V if it has enough charge.

Interconnection rules

Rule 1.

The battery will produce 3V for 8 hours if it is connected to one torchbulb; for 4 hours if it is connected to 2 torchbulbs; for $2\frac{2}{3}$ hours if it is connected to 3 torchbulbs, etc.

Rule 2.

If more than one torchbulb is connected to a battery, then they must be connected as shown in Figure 1.1.

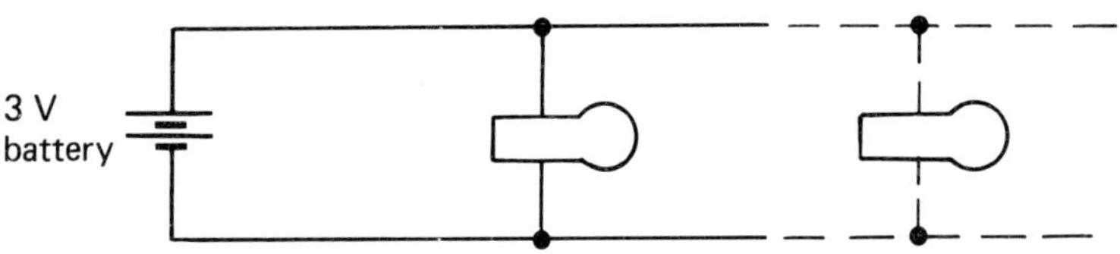

Figure 1.1. Torchbulb and battery connections

Functional requirements

The problem is to light 8 torchbulbs for $2\frac{1}{2}$ hours using a minimum number of batteries.

Solution

The solution is that you can connect 3 torchbulbs to each battery, which will produce the following solution, shown in Figure 1.2.

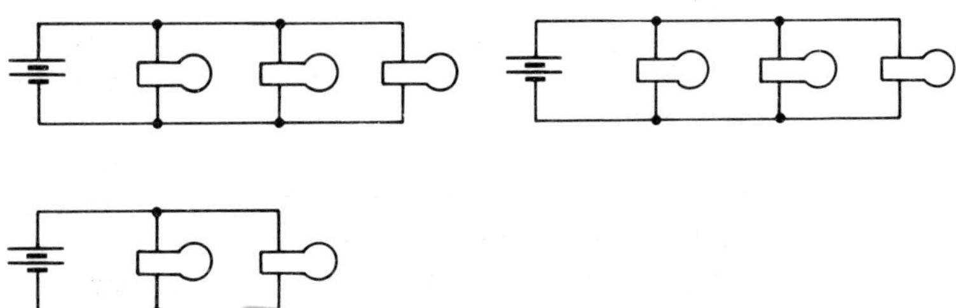

Figure 1.2. Solution to torchbulb problem

This example is a very simple one, but it illustrates the basic approach to hardware design.

1.2 NUMBERING SYSTEMS

We use the decimal, or base 10, system. It consists of the digits 0 to 9, i.e. 10 different digits. The reason we use the decimal system is that we have 10 fingers. Other numbering systems are possible. For instance, if we only had 7 fingers, we would probably count:

0
1
2
3
4
5
6
10
11
.
.
.
65
66
100
.
.

All our mathematics (well, most) is based on a numbering system which has 10 distinct states. If we only had 7 fingers, it would probably be based on 7 states.

The fundamental building blocks in digital design have only 2 states: On and Off. Hence a new system of numbering was needed for digital electronics—the binary, or base 2, system.

Table 1.1 is a conversion table between decimal and binary.

Each digit in the binary system is called a bit (BInary digiT). Hence the decimal number 10 corresponds to a 4 bit number.

Instead of writing decimal 10 or binary 1010 to distinguish between numbering systems, there are less clumsy ways to differentiate. One way is to put the base as a subscript after the number. Thus decimal 24 becomes 24_{10} and binary 1011 becomes 1011_2. This way is impractical when using computers, because they cannot normally use subscripts. The way computers distinguish between numbering systems is to place a letter after the number under question. A decimal number will have the letter D after it and a binary number will have the letter B after it.

Decimal	*Binary*
0	0
1	1
2	10
3	11
4	100
5	101
6	110
7	111
8	1000
9	1001
10	1010
11	1011
etc.	

Table 1.1 Decimal/Binary conversion table

Sometimes decimal numbers do not have any letter after them.

Hence $12 = 12_{10} = 12D = 1100_2 = 1100B$.

With the advent of computers, it was found to be convenient to group bits into blocks of 8. This is called a byte. Similarly 4 bits is called a nibble.

Historically, devices for getting information in and out of computers used nibbles. Hence a new numbering system was developed—the hexadecimal, or base 16, system. This system uses the first 6 letters of the alphabet, in addition to the decimal numbers. The advantage of this system is that binary information may be displayed in a more readily understandable form. Table 1.2 is a conversion table between decimal, binary, and hexadecimal.

Hexadecimal numbers are represented by an H after the number or, in some notations, by a # before the number.

Appendix A shows how to convert between decimal, binary and hexadecimal.

Decimal	*Binary*	*Hexadecimal*
0	0 0000	0
1	0 0001	1
2	0 0010	2
3	0 0011	3
4	0 0100	4
5	0 0101	5
6	0 0110	6
7	0 0111	7
8	0 1000	8
9	0 1001	9
10	0 1010	A
11	0 1011	B
12	0 1100	C
13	0 1101	D
14	0 1110	E
15	0 1111	F
16	1 0000	10
17	1 0001	11
18	1 0010	12
19	1 0011	13
20	1 0100	14

Table 1.2 Decimal/Binary/Hexadecimal conversion table

1.3 BOOLEAN ALGEBRA

Boolean Algebra is a set of rules which are ideally suited to digital circuits. The principle behind Boolean Algebra is that the solution of its equations are either true or false. The digit 1 is used to represent a true solution and the digit 0 is used to represent a false solution. The rules of Boolean Algebra are given in Appendix B, but some simple rules are shown below:

1. OR addition. If either Input A OR Input B is 1, then the output is 1.

a. $0 + 0 = 0$
b. $0 + 1 = 1$
c. $1 + 1 = 1$
d. $A + 1 = 1$
e. $A + 0 = A$
f. $A + A = A$
g. $A + \overline{A} = 1$ ($\overline{A}$ is the inverse of A. i.e. if $\overline{A}$ is 1, A is 0 and vice-versa)

Note: A + B may be written as AVB.

2. AND multiplication. If Input A AND Input B are 1, then the output is 1.

a. $0 \,.\, 0 = 0$
b. $0 \,.\, 1 = 0$
c. $1 \,.\, 1 = 1$
d. $A \,.\, 1 = A$
e. $A \,.\, 0 = 0$
f. $A \,.\, A = A$
g. $A \,.\, \overline{A} = 0$
Note: A . B may be written as AB or A^B.

3. NOT operation. The output is the inverse of the input.

a. $\overline{0} = 1$
b. $\overline{1} = 0$
Note: $\overline{A}$ may be written as ~A.

As will be seen in Chapter 2, there are digital circuits which correspond to the OR, AND and NOT functions. Boolean Algebra may be used to implement a circuit in the most efficient manner.

An example of how Boolean Algebra may be used is shown below:

Example

There are four shareholders in a company. Shareholder A has 46 per cent; shareholders B, C and D have 18 per cent each. The problem is to design a system whereby they can have secret ballots.

Solution

The first thing to do is to write down all the possible ways that the motion may be carried (assume that abstaining is not allowed).

1. Shareholder A and at least one other shareholder votes yes.
2. Shareholders B, C and D all vote yes.

These two ways may be rewritten in Boolean format as:

1. A.(B+C+D)	A votes yes AND (EITHER B OR C OR D vote yes)
2. B.C.D	B votes yes AND C votes yes AND D votes yes.

Hence the Boolean expression for the motion to be carried may be written as A(B+C+D)+BCD.

An implementation of this circuit is shown in Chapter 2.

1.4 TRUTH TABLES

A truth table is a combination of all of the possible inputs and their effect on the output(s) of a digital circuit. The truth table for the OR function is given in Table 1.3.

A	*B*	*Output*
0	0	0
0	1	1
1	0	1
1	1	1

Table 1.3 Truth table for the OR function

Alternatively you can use F (for False) instead of 0 and T (for True) instead of 1. This is an equally valid way of displaying a truth table. Digital circuits operate on voltage levels which can be represented by H (for High) and L (for Low). Normally H corresponds to logic 1 and L to logic 0. This is known as positive logic and is used throughout this book. However, there is another method known as negative logic which has H corresponding to logic 0 and L corresponding to logic 1. Table 1.4 shows the different ways of representing the AND function.

A	*B*	*Output*	*A*	*B*	*Output*	*A*	*B*	*Output*	*A*	*B*	*Output*
0	0	0	F	F	F	L	L	L	H	H	H
0	1	0	F	T	F	L	H	L	H	L	H
1	0	0	T	F	F	H	L	L	L	H	H
1	1	1	T	T	T	H	H	H	L	L	L

a. Logic 0 and 1, b. True/False, c. Positive logic, d. Negative logic.

Table 1.4 Four ways of representing the truth table for the AND function

1.5 CONCLUSION

The principles outlined in this chapter are used throughout the book. All hardware designers should be aware of Boolean Algebra, numbering systems, etc.

1.6 SUMMARY

There are two numbering systems that are used in digital design:

Binary	(Base 2)
Hexadecimal	(Base 16).

Boolean Algebra is a set of rules which are useful in digital design. These rules centre around three main functions:

OR function
AND function
NOT function.

2
Basic Building Blocks

2.1 INTRODUCTION

This chapter will explain what the basic building blocks of hardware are and how they are used. It will then go on to explain slightly more complicated blocks which may be created by connecting the most basic blocks together.

2.2 AND, OR AND NOT GATES

These are three of the most simple building blocks involved in digital design.

2.2.1 AND gate

This gate will give a logic high or "true" output if all of its inputs are true; i.e. if Input A AND Input B AND Input C, etc. are true, then the output will be true.

The truth table for a 2 input AND gate is shown in Table 2.1 and the circuit symbol is shown in Figure 2.1.

The output is represented by A.B or AB in Boolean format.

Input A	*Input B*	*Output*
0	0	0
0	1	0
1	0	0
1	1	1

Table 2.1 Truth table for a 2 input AND gate

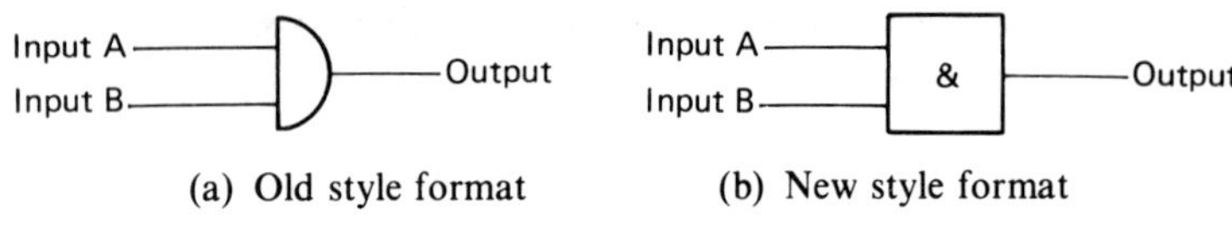

(a) Old style format (b) New style format

Figure 2.1 Circuit symbols for a 2 input AND gate

What I have labelled as the new style format is now becoming the standard way of showing logic gates—this way should be used by the reader since it is a more comprehensive method. The old style format was and is widely used; hence a knowledge of it is essential. This book will jump between the two formats to give the reader confidence in both.

2.2.2 OR gate

This gate will give a logic high or "true" output if any of its inputs are true; i.e. IF Input A OR Input B OR Input C, etc. are true, then the output will be true.

The truth table for a 2 input OR gate is shown in Table 2.2 and the circuit symbol is shown in Figure 2.2.

The output is represented by A+B in Boolean format.

Input A	*Input B*	*Output*
0	0	0
0	1	1
1	0	1
1	1	1

Table 2.2 Truth table for a 2 input OR gate

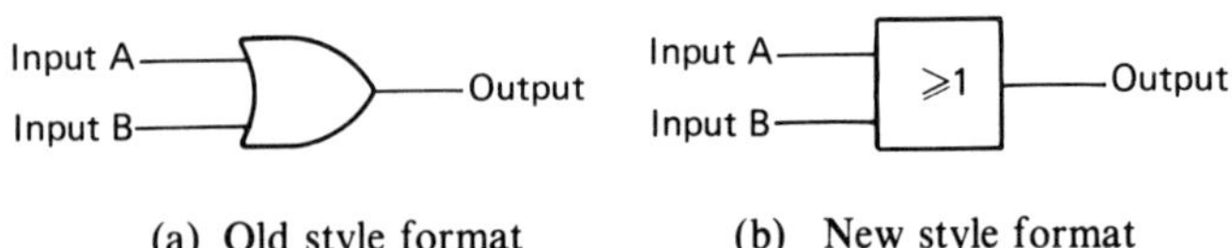

(a) Old style format (b) New style format

Figure 2.2 Circuit symbols for a 2 input OR gate

2.2.3 NOT gate

This gate will invert its input; i.e. if the input is true, then the output will be false and vice-versa. The truth table for the NOT gate is shown

in Table 2.3 and the circuit symbol is shown in Figure 2.3.
The output is represented by $\overline{A}$ in Boolean format.

Input	*Output*
0	1
1	0

Table 2.3 Truth table for the NOT gate

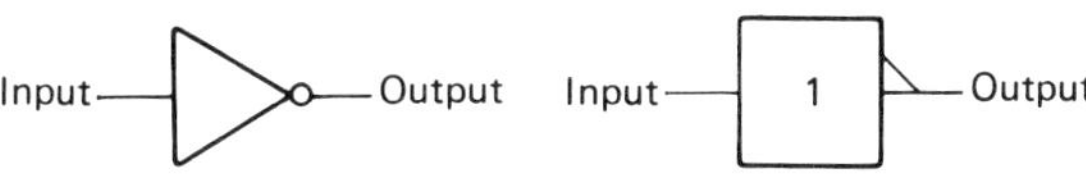

(a) Old style format (b) New style format

Figure 2.3 Circuit symbols for the NOT gate

2.3 COMBINING SIMPLE GATES

These simple gates may be combined in various ways to produce four more, very useful, gates.

2.3.1 NAND gate

This is merely an AND gate with its output inverted by a NOT gate. The combination is shown in Figure 2.4. The truth table is shown in Table 2.4 and its circuit symbol is shown in Figure 2.5.

The output is represented by $\overline{A.B}$ or $\overline{AB}$ in Boolean format.

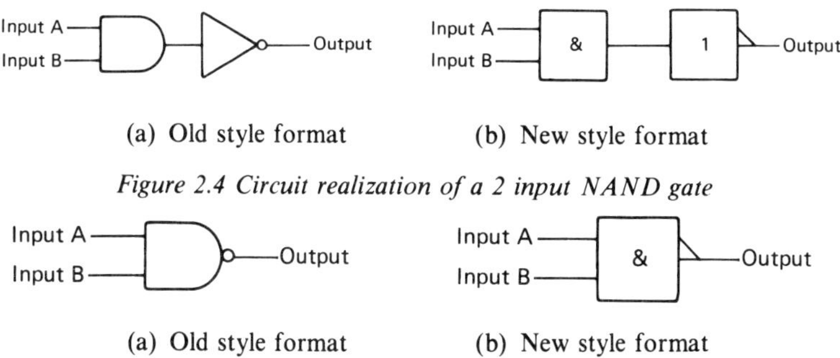

(a) Old style format (b) New style format

Figure 2.4 Circuit realization of a 2 input NAND gate

(a) Old style format (b) New style format

Figure 2.5 Circuit symbols for a 2 input NAND gate

Input A	*Input B*	*Output*
0	0	1
0	1	1
1	0	1
1	1	0

Table 2.4 Truth table for a 2 input NAND gate

2.3.2 NOR gate

This is an OR gate with its output inverted by a NOT gate. The combination is shown in Figure 2.6. The truth table is shown in Table 2.5 and the circuit symbol is shown in Figure 2.7.

The output is represented by $\overline{A+B}$ in Boolean format.

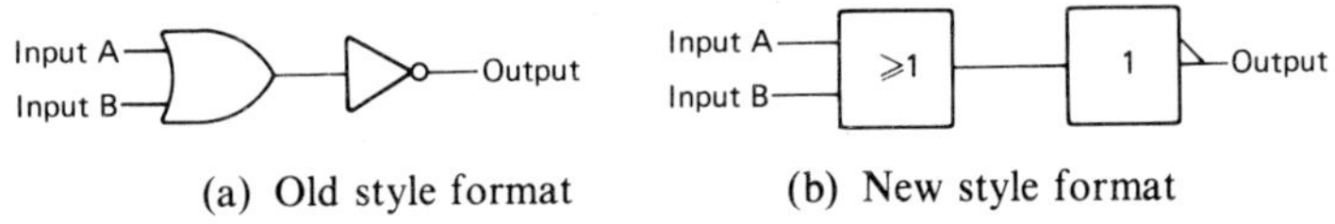

(a) Old style format (b) New style format

Figure 2.6 Circuit realization of a 2 input NOR gate

Input A	*Input B*	*Output*
0	0	1
0	1	0
1	0	0
1	1	0

Table 2.5 Truth table for a 2 input NOR gate

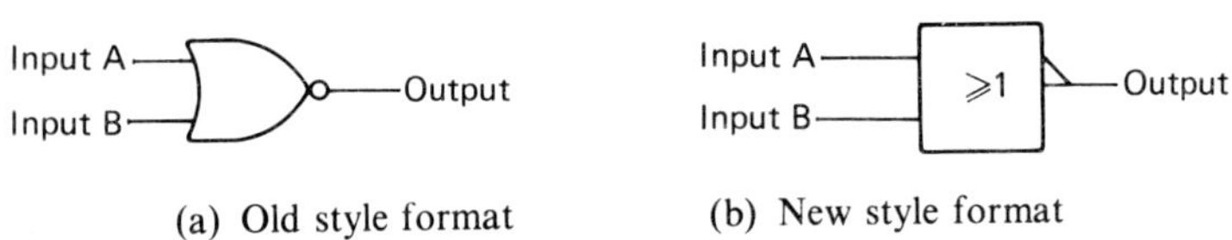

(a) Old style format (b) New style format

Figure 2.7 Circuit symbols for a 2 input NOR gate

2.3.3 Exclusive OR gate (XOR)

This gate gives a true output if either of its inputs are true, but not if both inputs are true. One way of producing an XOR gate is shown in Figure 2.8. The truth table is shown in Table 2.6 and the circuit symbol is shown in Figure 2.9.

The output is represented by $A \oplus B$ in Boolean format.

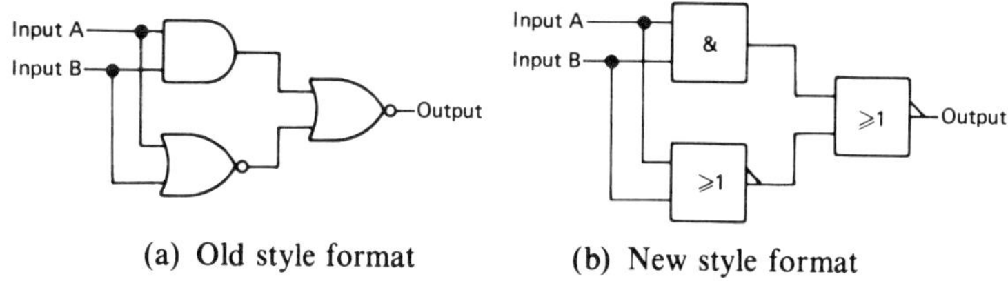

(a) Old style format (b) New style format

Figure 2.8 Circuit realization of an XOR gate

Input A	*Input B*	*Output*
0	0	0
0	1	1
1	0	1
1	1	0

Table 2.6 Truth table for an XOR gate

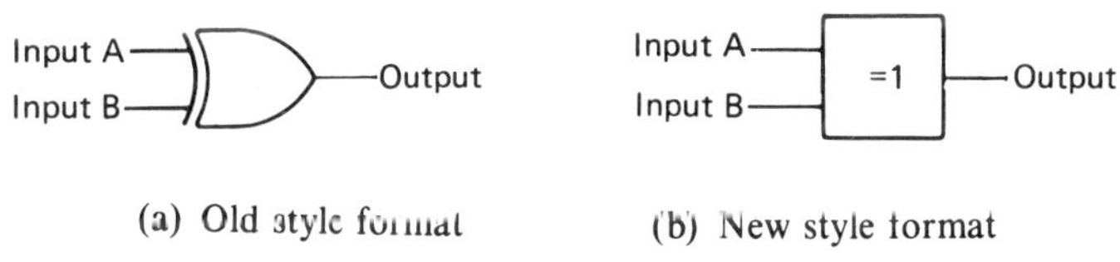

(a) Old style format (b) New style format

Figure 2.9 Circuit symbols for an XOR gate

2.3.4 Exclusive NOR gate (XNOR)

This is the inverse of the XOR gate. Its output is represented by $\overline{A \oplus B}$ in Boolean format and its circuit symbol is shown in Figure 2.10.

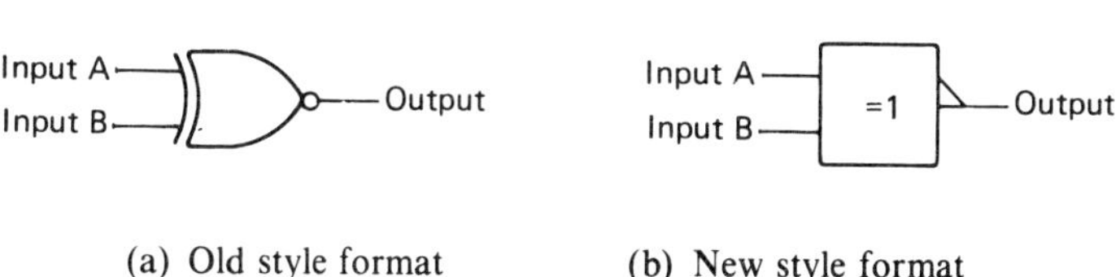

(a) Old style format (b) New style format

Figure 2.10 Circuit symbols for an XNOR gate

Exercise

All of the gates produced in this chapter may be generated from either NAND or NOR gates. Produce circuits to do this.

2.4 MULTIPLE INPUT GATES

All of the gates mentioned so far have two inputs (except for the NOT gate). This is the most common number of inputs. However it is possible to have any number of inputs to a gate.

2.5 PRACTICAL EXAMPLE

Now, let us design a circuit to solve the voting problem described in Chapter 1.

The Boolean expression for the motion was A(B+C+D)+BCD.

Figure 2.11 shows a circuit whose function is the same as the Boolean expression.

The solution will be logic 1 if the motion is carried.

Chapter 3 will show how this circuit can be built, using widely available components.

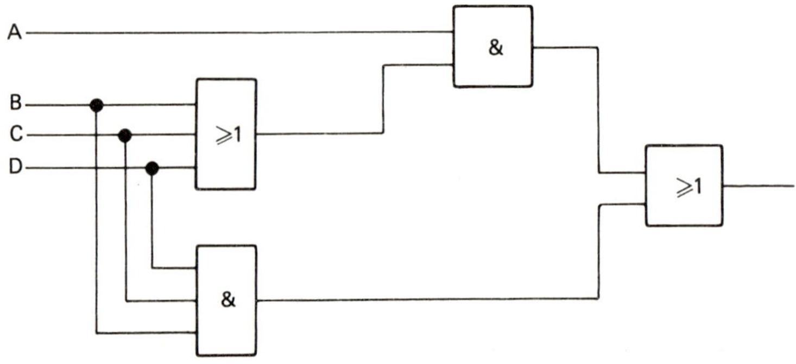

*Figure 2.11 Circuit representation of A(B+*C+D)+BCD

2.6 DEMORGAN'S THEOREMS

The logic gates shown above may be used in many applications. For instance an OR gate may be viewed as having an output of 1 if at least one input is 1. Another, equally valid, way of looking at the OR gate is to say that the output will be 0 if all of the inputs are 0. Both ways define the OR gate.

To understand why it is a good idea to define the OR gate in two ways, read the following.

If you wanted to design a circuit with the Boolean function $\overline{\overline{A}.\overline{B}}$, then you could use two NOT gates and a NAND gate. This would give the correct result. However, if you do the truth table for this function, as shown in Figure 2.7, then you can see that the truth table for $\overline{\overline{A}.\overline{B}}$ is the same as for A+B—the OR function. Hence $\overline{\overline{A}.\overline{B}}$=A+B. In a similar manner, $\overline{\overline{A}+\overline{B}}$=A.B.

A	B	$\overline{A}$	$\overline{B}$	$\overline{A}.\overline{B}$	$\overline{\overline{A}\,\overline{B}}$	A+B
0	0	1	1	1	0	0
0	1	1	0	0	1	1
1	0	0	1	0	1	1
1	1	0	0	0	1	1

Table 2.7 Truth table for $\overline{\overline{A}.\overline{B}}$

DeMorgan was the first person to formulate these two equations and hence they are known as DeMorgan's Theorems.

The AND, NAND, OR and NOR gates may be represented in two ways—by the normal method, or by their DeMorgan equivalent.

For instance, the NAND function may be written as $\overline{A.B}$ or $\overline{A}+\overline{B}$. The circuit symbol of the DeMorgan equivalent is given in Figure 2.12.

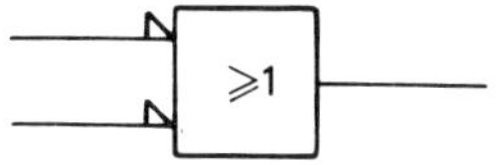

Figure 2.12 DeMorgan equivalent for a NAND gate

The symbol in Figure 2.12 may be translated as follows:

IF Input A is 0 OR Input B is 0 (or both), THEN the output will be 1. If there had been a triangle on the output line, then the symbol would represent an AND gate.

DeMorgan equivalents are used in circuit diagrams to aid comprehension of how the circuit works. This may not be clear now, but it will become more clear as you read on.

2.7 EXPLANATION OF NEW LOGIC SYMBOLS

The new logic symbols enable you to determine the function of a device without having to look at the truth table or internal logic. They are explained in detail in the TTL data book (Texas Instruments) and will be covered as they appear in this book.

The basic symbol is the box, with inputs and outputs. The symbols seen so far are those for the AND, OR, NOT, NAND, NOR, XOR and XNOR gates. The AND gate had 2 lines into the box, a & in the box and one line coming out of the box. This means that the Output=Input 1 AND Input 2.

The OR gate had 2 lines into the box, a ⩾1 in the box and one line coming out of the box. This means that the Output = Input 1 OR Input 2.

The NOT gate had one line into the box, a 1 in the box and one line coming out of the box *with a triangle on it*. The triangle means that the output is active low (as opposed to active high). Hence the active high input is passed through the gate and since the output is active low, it is inverted.

The NAND gate is the same as the AND gate, except that it has a triangle on its output. This means that the output is active low and so it is inverted.

The NOR gate is the same as the OR gate, except that it has a triangle on its output and hence has an active low output.

The XOR gate has two lines into the box, a =1 in the box and one line coming out of the box. This means that the Output = Input 1 XOR Input 2.

The XNOR gate is the same as the XOR gate, except that it has a triangle on its output and hence has an active low output.

2.8 CONCLUSION

These building, or logic, blocks may be combined to produce many different digital devices. Some of these devices are shown in Chapter 4. Most designs that the reader will do will incorporate some of the basic logic blocks.

2.9 SUMMARY

The devices covered in this chapter, along with their circuit symbols and Boolean expressions, are:

Device	*Old style symbol*	*New style symbol*	*DeMorgan equivalent*	*Boolean expression*
AND	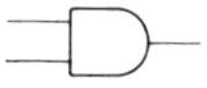	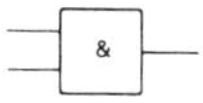 &	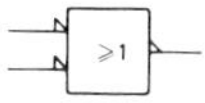 ≥1	A.B or AB (or $\overline{\bar{A}+\bar{B}}$)
OR		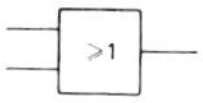 ≥1	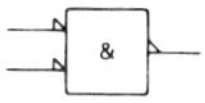 &	A+B (or $\overline{\bar{A}.\bar{B}}$)
NOT		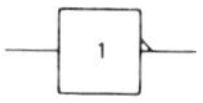 1	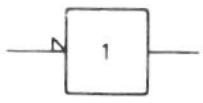 1	A
NAND	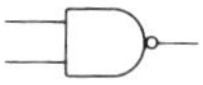	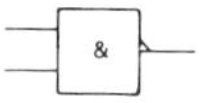 &	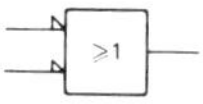 ≥1	$\overline{A.B}$ or $\overline{AB}$ (or A+B)
NOR		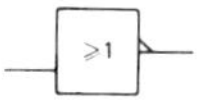 ≥1	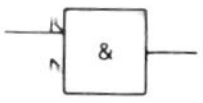 &	A+B (or $\bar{A}.\bar{B}$)
XOR		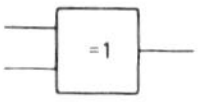 =1		$A \oplus B$
XNOR	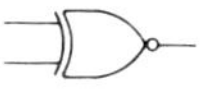	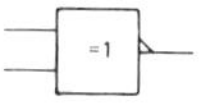 =1		$\overline{A \oplus B}$

Either the old-style or new-style symbols may be used in circuit diagrams. The new-style symbols are becoming the standard set.

These devices form the basis of a great many more complicated devices.

3
Making Your Own Circuits

This chapter explains what you need to do to make your own circuits.

3.1 GENERAL EQUIPMENT

Table 3.1 is a list of necessary tools/equipment (with approximate 1985 prices) for someone doing practical work. Not all of these are necessary for building the circuits in this book, but they are all useful to have.

Soldering iron	£15
Multicore solder	£1 per 10 m
Solder sucker/Desoldering tool	£6
Long-nosed pliers	£6
Wire cutters	£4
Wire strippers	£3
Multimeter	£30
Veroboard spot face cutter	£2
Breadboard	£8
Solid core wire	£2 per 100 m
Stranded core wire	£2 per 100 m
Assorted sizes of veroboard	£3 each
+5V power supply	£35 for a 1A linear supply

Table 3.1 List of necessary tools with approximate 1985 prices

Examples of each of the tools in Table 3.1 are shown in the photographs (Plates 1–7).

Veroboard (sometimes known as stripboard) consists of copper tracks bonded to an insulating board with holes in the tracks to accept IC pins or discrete component pins (see Chapter 5—Analog

Plate 1 Veroboard and veroboard spot face cutter

components). The type of veroboard used with Integrated Circuits has 0.1″ pitch holes, each 1 mm in diameter.

Note: Components should be put in the component side of the veroboard.

The veroboard spot face cutter can cut the copper tracks, allowing a customized circuit to be made.

Eurocards are a specialized type of veroboard. They are more useful than normal veroboard for designs with ICs (as opposed to discrete devices—transistors, capacitors, resistors, etc.), although discrete devices can be used with Eurocards. It is seldom necessary to cut the tracks on Eurocards.

A *soldering iron* is needed to connect ICs, discrete devices and wires to veroboards, etc. The technique of soldering components is not very difficult:

Plate 2 Eurocard.

1. Place component in veroboard component side.
2. Turn veroboard over and gently bend one or two pins on the component to prevent it from falling out.
3. Ensure that the soldering iron is hot enough to melt solder and is not covered in flux/dirt (a damp cloth is very good for cleaning soldering irons).
4. Touch the soldering iron to the pin you want to solder.
5. Touch the solder to the pin after a second or two (to allow the pin to warm up).
6. Remove the soldering iron and solder.

The object of soldering is to get a permanent electrical connection between a component and a veroboard (or similar). Two points to consider are:

a. If you don't hold the soldering iron to the pin for long enough, you may not get a good solder connection (dry joint). These are usually noticeable by the rough look of the solder (good connections are smooth and shiny).

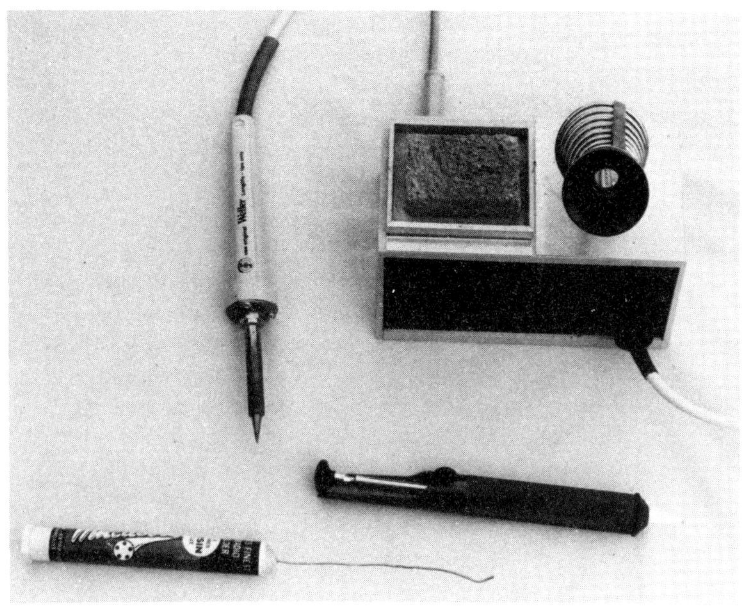

Plate 3 Soldering iron, solder and desoldering tool.

b. If you hold a very powerful soldering iron to a pin for too long, it may damage the component. This is unlikely to happen with a low-powered soldering iron, but it is a point to remember.

The soldering iron should be between 20W and 50W, with a No. 7 bit. (The higher the rating in watts, the faster a soldering iron will heat up. Different bits work at different temperatures.)

The solder should be *multicore tin lead solder*—thickness 22 SWG (Standard Wire Gauge).

To use the *desoldering tool*, press the lever down, heat up the joint with a soldering iron and press the lever release button. This creates a partial vacuum which sucks the solder off the joint.

Long-nosed pliers are used for fiddly jobs which require the dexterity of fingers, but in places that fingers cannot reach.

Wire cutters have an obvious use.

Wire strippers are used to strip the insulation off wires, so that the bare metal can be soldered, connected, etc.

The advantage of *solid core wire* is that there is only one wire to connect to the veroboard, etc. when making connections. When you use stranded core wire, you have to twist the wires together and then "tin" them with solder (touch a soldering iron to the wire and put some solder on). This makes it easier to put stranded core wire through veroboard holes. The advantage of *stranded core* wire is that it is much more flexible. If you bend a solid core wire too often, it will snap. It is very difficult to snap a stranded core wire this way.

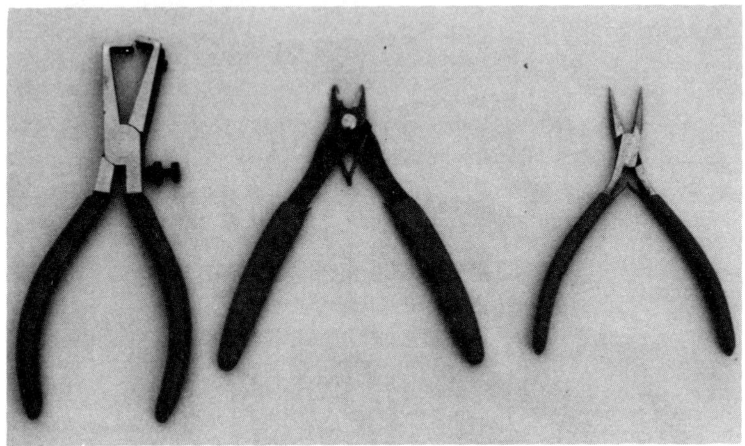

Plate 4 Long-nosed pliers, wire cutters and wirestrippers

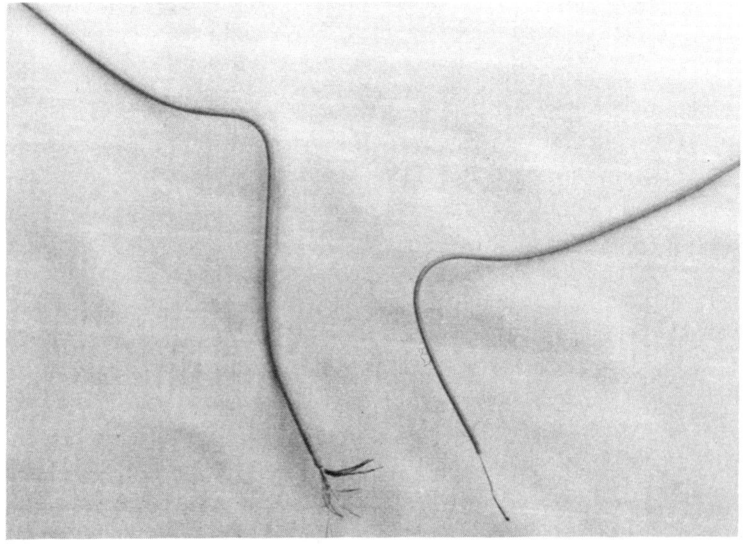

Plate 5 Solid core and stranded core wire

Hence solid core wires are normally used for connections on a veroboard and stranded core wires are normally used for connections in between veroboards, etc.

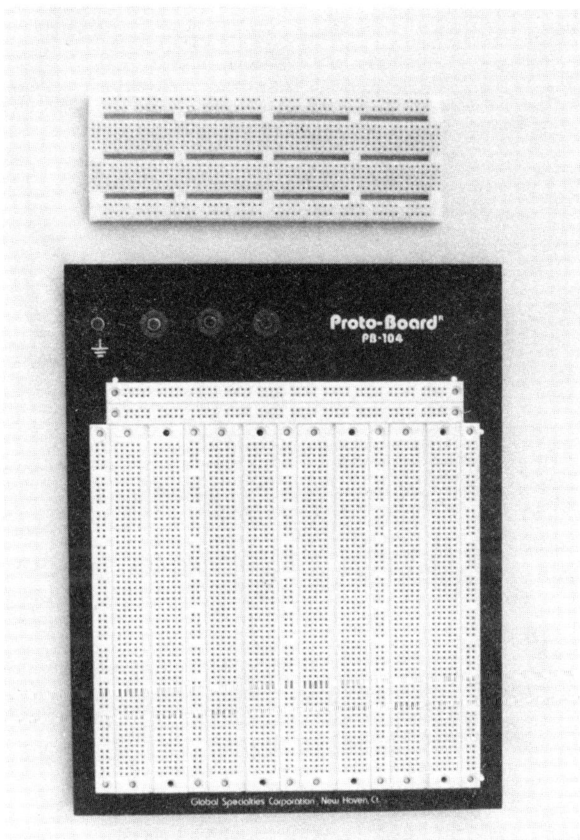

Plate 6 Two breadboards

Breadboards allow you to test a circuit without any soldering. The holes are usually connected in groups of four or five. This gives a similar layout to that used for Eurocards. When using breadboards, it is best to use solid core wire because it is difficult to force stranded core wire into the holes.

A *multimeter* is a device which allows you to measure resistance, voltage and current. Hence it may be used to test if a connection is made in a circuit (if it is, there should be 0 ohms resistance between the two ends of the connection).

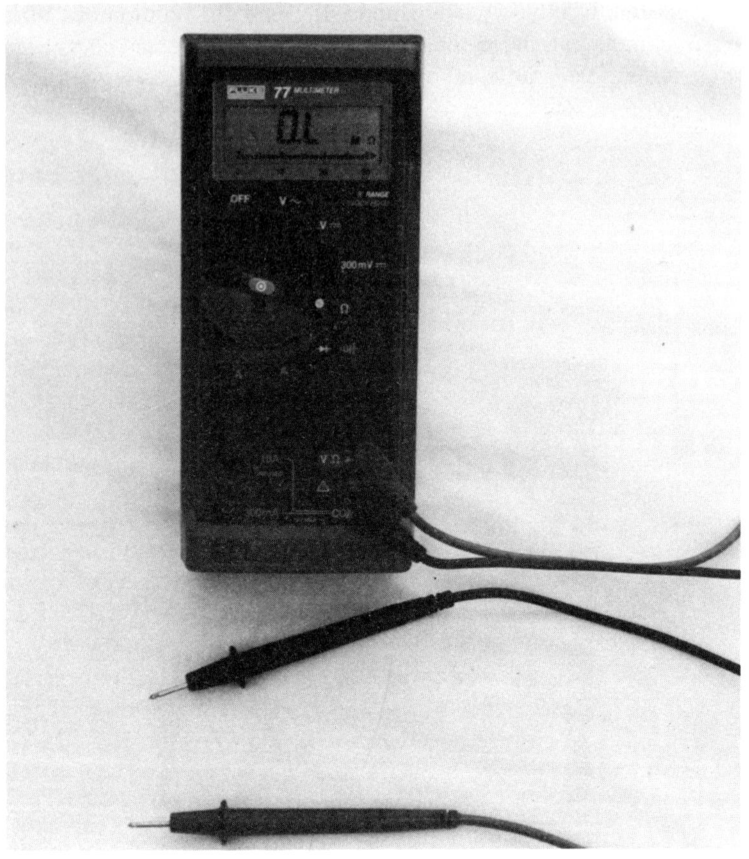

Plate 7 Multimeter

These tools can be obtained from many sources. Maplin are one of the best sources of tools and equipment for the consumer (electronics companies use Verospeed, Macro Marketing, RS, etc.) and their catalogue is available from W.H. Smith and other newsagents or electronics shops. The head office of Maplin is:

P.O. Box 3
Rayleigh
Essex
SS6 8LR

Phone (0702) 554155

Although Maplin do sell components, as well as equipment, there are two companies, Technomatic and Watford Electronics, who have a much wider range of components. Most electronics magazines have advertisements for either or both of these companies which give a sizeable list of their available components and prices. Their addresses are:

Technomatic	Watford Electronics
17 Burnley Road	35/37 Cardiff Road
London	Watford
NW10 1ED	Herts
Phone (01) 452 1500	Phone (0923) 40588

3.2 BASIC TTL

TTL, or Transistor-Transistor Logic, is a method of producing circuit components. The TTL range of components is extensive and is easy to use. Texas Instruments produce the 74 series of TTL devices, as do many other manufacturers.

TTL devices are produced in DIL (Dual In Line) packages (also known as DIPs) as are most digital components (see Plate 8). These DIPs have an even number of pins, usually between 6 and 64. The DIP contains an Integrated Circuit (IC) which performs the particular TTL function. The logic gates described in Chapter 2 are all produced in TTL and a brief description of each follows:

Plate 8 16 pin DIP

3.2.1 2 input AND gate

4 AND gates are packaged in a 14 pin DIP, as shown in Figure 3.1.

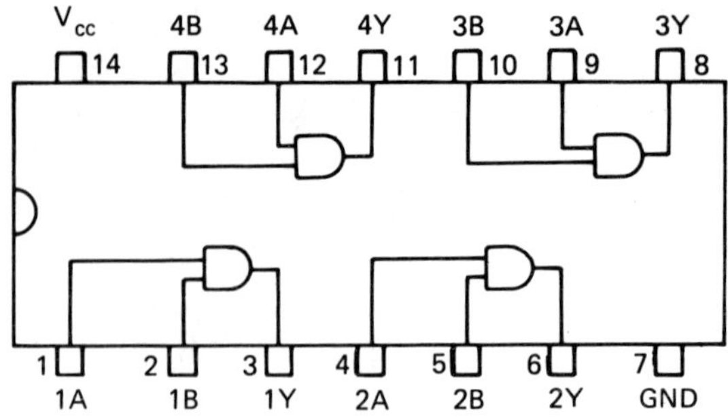

Figure 3.1 Diagram of a Quad 2 input AND gate

Vcc is +5V and GND is 0V. These two inputs supply power to make the gates work.

The notch on the left of the DIP indicates the orientation of the DIP. Pin 1 is always the pin below the notch when the notch is on the left hand side. *It is important to remember this because if you get it wrong, the IC tends to stop working.*

The number of this component is 7408.
Approximate cost is 14p.

3.2.2 2 input OR gate

4 OR gates are packaged in a 14 pin DIP, as shown in Figure 3.2.

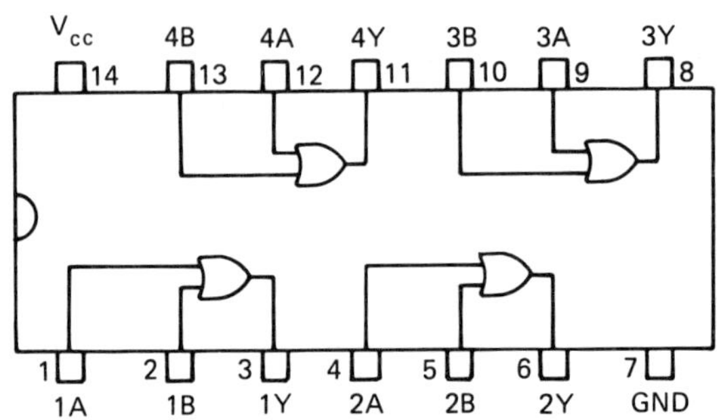

Figure 3.2 Diagram of a Quad 2 input OR gate

The number of this component is 7432.
Approximate cost is 14p.

3.2.3 NOT gate

6 NOT gates are packaged in a 14 pin DIP, as shown in Figure 3.3.

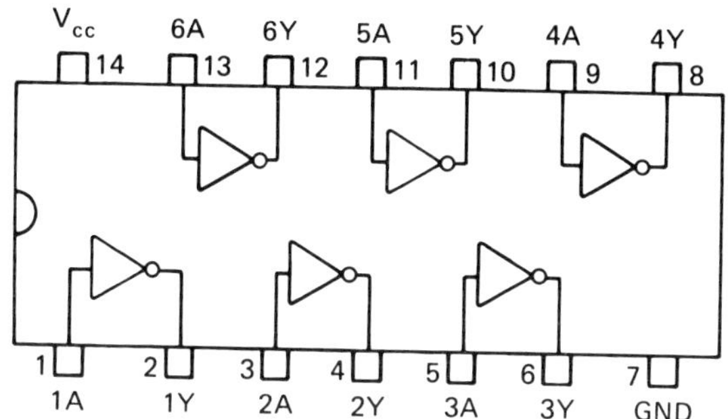

Figure 3.3 Diagram of a hex NOT gate

The number of this component is 7404.
Approximate cost is 12p.

3.2.4 2 input NAND gate

4 NAND gates are packaged in a 14 pin DIP, as shown in Figure 3.4.

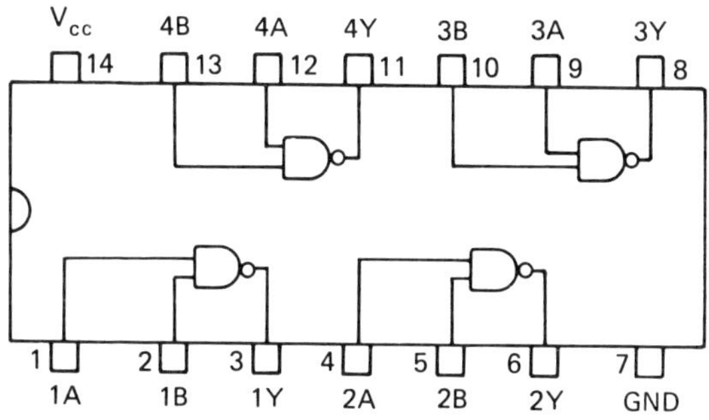

Figure 3.4 Diagram of a Quad 2 input NAND gate

The number of this component is 7400.
Approximate cost is 11p.

3.2.5 2 input NOR gate

4 NOR gates are packaged in a 14 pin DIP, as shown in Figure 3.5.

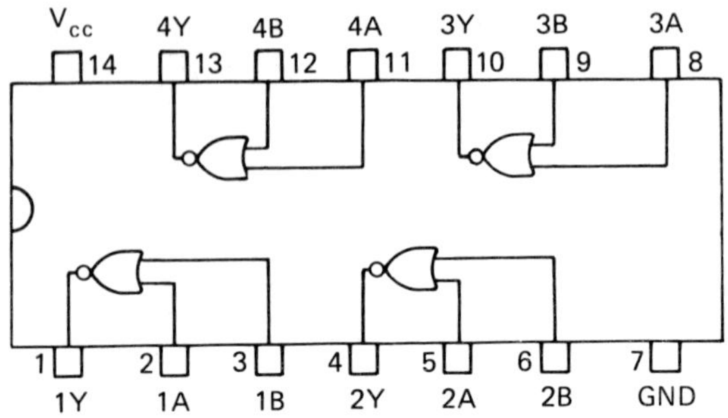

Figure 3.5 Diagram of a Quad 2 input NOR gate

The number of this component is 7402.
Approximate cost is 12p.

3.2.6 XOR gate

4 XOR gates are packaged in a 14 pin DIP, as shown in Figure 3.6.

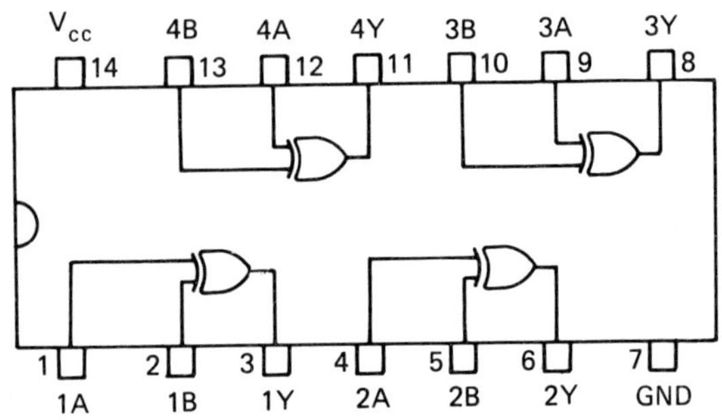

Figure 3.6 Diagram of a Quad XOR gate

The number of this component is 7486.
Approximate cost is 16p.

3.2.7 2 input XNOR gate

4 XNOR gates are packaged in a 14 pin DIP, as shown in Figure 3.7.

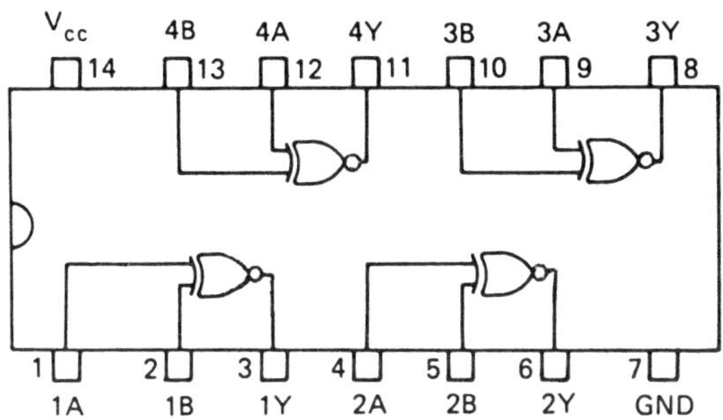

Figure 3.7 Diagram of a Quad 2 input XNOR gate

The number of this component is 74266.
Approximate cost is 50p.

3.2.8 3 input AND gate

3 AND gates are packaged in a 14 pin DIP, as shown in Figure 3.8.

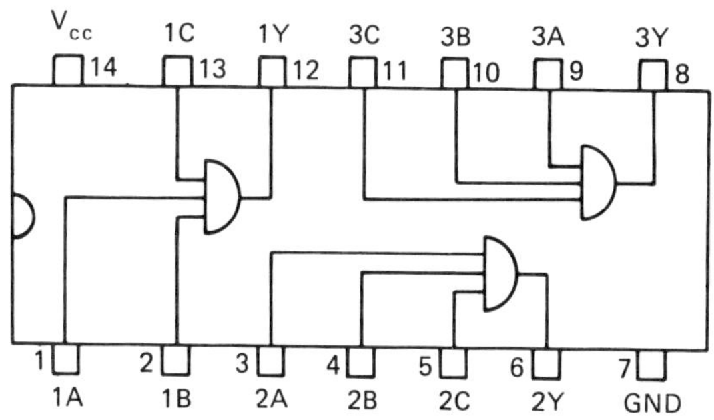

Figure 3.8 Diagram of a triple 3 input AND gate

The number of this component is 7411.
Approximate cost is 16p.

3.3 USING BASIC TTL

If you have a circuit which contains four 2 input NAND gates, then only one 7400 will be required to implement that part of the circuit. If you have five 2 input NAND gates, then two 7400s will be required. The other three NAND gates in the second package may be used as NOT gates (by tying their inputs together) or just not used.

Back to the voting problem from Chapters 1 and 2.

3 input OR gates are not made in TTL and so two 2 input OR gates will be used instead, which gives the circuit in Figure 3.9.

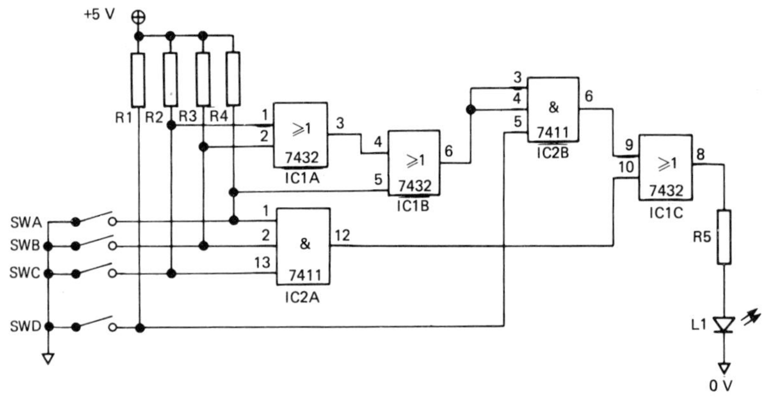

Figure 3.9 Practical solution to the voting problem

Explanation of Figure 3.9:

SWA-SWD	are single pole single throw switches (on/off).
R1-R4	are pull up resistors. They ensure that there is a known voltage (+5V) on the inputs to the gates if any switch is in the off position. Their value is 4700 ohms. The reason for this value will become clear in Chapter 6. Without the resistors, when a switch was opened, +5V would short to 0V and the power supply could be broken.
IC1	is a 7432 Quad 2 input OR gate. A, B and C represent the different gates within the package. The numbers above the lines are the pin numbers in the package.

IC2 is a 7411. The reason why IC2B has 2 inputs tied together is that it is being used as a 2 input AND gate (it is more efficient to have one 7411 with one gate unused than to have one 7411 with two gates unused and an extra 7408 with three gates unused).

L1 is a Light Emitting Diode (LED). LEDs will be discussed in Chapter 5. LEDs tend to burn out if too much current passes through them, and so R5 is used to limit the current passing through the LED. The LED will glow if current is passing through it, i.e. if IC1's output is high.

R5 limits current through L1. Its value is 4700 ohms.

All of these components may be bought from the companies previously mentioned.

Exercise

Build the circuit shown in Figure 3.9 on the breadboard.

Exercise

Build the circuit shown in Figure 3.9 using veroboard. Make sure that you cut any unwanted connections using the veroboard spot face cutter.

3.4 CONCLUSION

After reading this chapter, you should be confident enough to design and build a circuit using simple TTL devices (the circuit on the veroboard is proof enough of your abilities). Practical examples in later chapters will assume that this chapter has been read and understood.

3.5 SUMMARY

The ICs covered in this chapter are:

7408	Quad 2 input AND gate
7432	Quad 2 input OR gate
7404	Hex NOT gate
7400	Quad 2 input NAND gate
7402	Quad 2 input NOR gate
7486	Quad XOR gate
74266	Quad XNOR gate
7411	Triple 3 input AND gate

4
More Complex Devices

This chapter deals with flip flops, shift registers and counters. All of these devices may be produced by combining the devices shown in previous chapters. Appendix C shows how these devices are made.

The outputs of the devices shown previously only depend upon the current state of their inputs. This is known as combinational logic. The outputs of the devices shown in this chapter depend, in part, on previous inputs. This is known as sequential logic.

4.1 CLOCKS

Sequential logic usually has a clock input which needs to be in the correct state before the output(s) will change.

A clock is a signal which changes state from a 1 to a 0 and vice-versa periodically, as demonstrated in Figure 4.1.

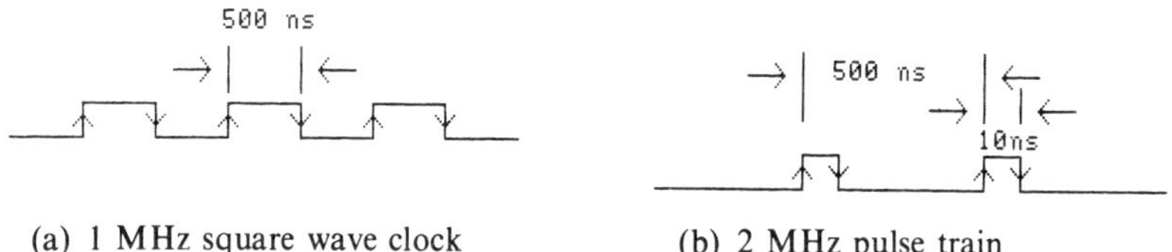

(a) 1 MHz square wave clock

(b) 2 MHz pulse train

Figure 4.1 Two examples of a clock signal

Figure 4.1 (a) shows a 1 MHz square wave clock. Every 500 ns (500×10^{-9} seconds), the clock signal is inverted.

Figure 4.1 (b) shows a 2 MHz pulse train. Every 500 ns there is a positive-going pulse which lasts 10 ns.

In both of these cases, the process is repeated *ad infinitum*.

Clock signals may be produced in many ways—some of these are described in Chapter 5.

Sequential logic operates on either the rising, or positive, edge (upward arrow shown in Figure 4.1) or the falling, or negative, edge (downward arrow shown in Figure 4.1) of a clock. An IC which operates on the rising edge of a clock is said to be triggered, or toggled, on the rising edge.

Some terms you are likely to come across in relation to clocks are:

Frequency
: This is the speed at which the clock changes from high to low to high again. It is measured in cycles per second (Hertz or Hz for short).

Period
: This is the reciprocal of the frequency and is the time taken for the clock to change from high to low to high again. It is measured in seconds.

Table 4.1 gives a list of frequencies and periods, using the common hardware notation.

Frequency	*Period*
1 Hz	1 s
10 Hz	100 ms (10^{-1} s)
100 Hz	10 ms (10^{-2} s)
1 kHz (10^3 Hz)	1 ms (10^{-3} s)
10 kHz (10^4 Hz)	100 us (10^{-4} s)
100 kHz (10^5 Hz)	10 us (10^{-5} s)
1 MHz (10^6 Hz)	1 us (10^{-6} s)
10 MHz (10^7 Hz)	100 ns (10^{-7} s)
100 MHz (10^8 Hz)	10 ns (10^{-8} s)
1 GHz (10^9 Hz)	1 ns (10^{-9} s)
10 GHz (10^{10} Hz)	100 ps (10^{-10} s)

Table 4.1 List of frequencies and periods

Note:

m is short for milli (10^{-3})
μ is short for micro (10^{-6})
n is short for nano (10^{-9})
p is short for pico (10^{-12})
k is short for kilo (10^3)

M is short for Mega (10^6)
G is short for Giga (10^9)

4.2 J-K FLIP FLOP

This is a simple storage element, which has 4 functions:

1. J=1, K=1
   If the output is a 1 (high), then when the clock input triggers, the output changes to a 0.
   If the output is a 0, it will change to a 1.
2. J=0, K=1
   When the clock triggers, the output changes to a 0.
3. J=1, K=0
   When the clock triggers, the output changes to a 1.
4. J=0, K=0
   When the clock triggers, the output remains the same as it was.

The truth table for the J-K flip flop is shown in Table 4.2 and the circuit representation in Figure 4.2.

Q is the non inverted output
$\bar{Q}$ is the inverted output

The clock input shows that the flip flop is triggered, or toggled, on the rising edge of the clock signal. Figure 4.3 shows the circuit representation of a flip flop which toggles on the falling edge of the clock signal.

J	*K*	*Q output after clock trigger*
0	0	Qn−1
0	1	0
1	0	1
1	1	$\bar{Q}$n−1

Table 4.2 Truth table for J-K flip flop

Note: Qn−1 is the Q output before the clock signal.

Explanation of new logic symbol

The symbol is self explanatory except for the >C. When an input has a >, then it is a clock input (it normally has a C as well to indicate that it is a control input).

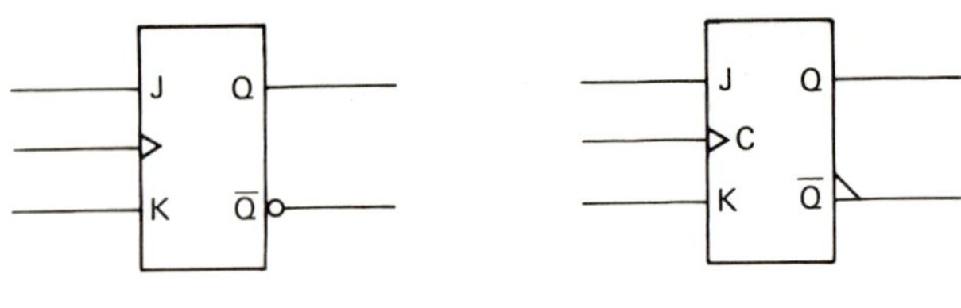

(a) Old style format (b) New style format

Figure 4.2 J-K flip flop representation

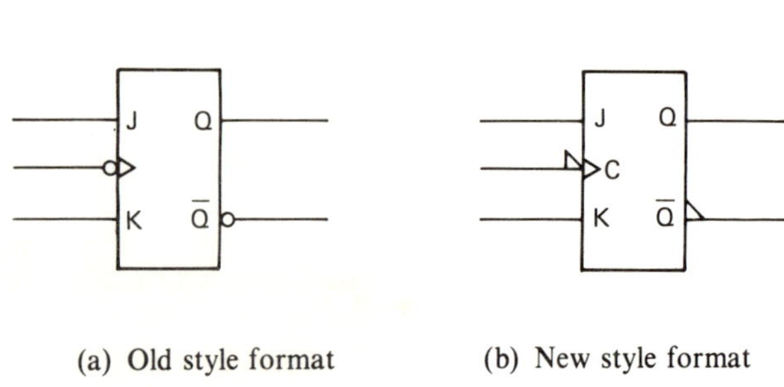

(a) Old style format (b) New style format

Figure 4.3 J-K flip flop which toggles on falling edge of clock

Hence to store a logic 1 in a J-K flip flop, you would do the following:

Set J=1 and K=0.
Trigger the clock input.
Set J=0 and K=0.

This would store 1 on the Q output. In hardware terms you would say that a logic 1 has been latched.

4.3 D TYPE FLIP FLOP

The J-K flip flop may be used as a storage device by cascading two or more together (see Figure 4.4). However, it would be nice to have a device which merely latched whatever was on its input to its output on receipt of a clock toggle. This can be done, using a J-K flip flop, as shown in Figure 4.5. Also shown in Figure 4.5 is the circuit representation of a D type flip flop. The extra signals are explained in the truth table in Table 4.3.

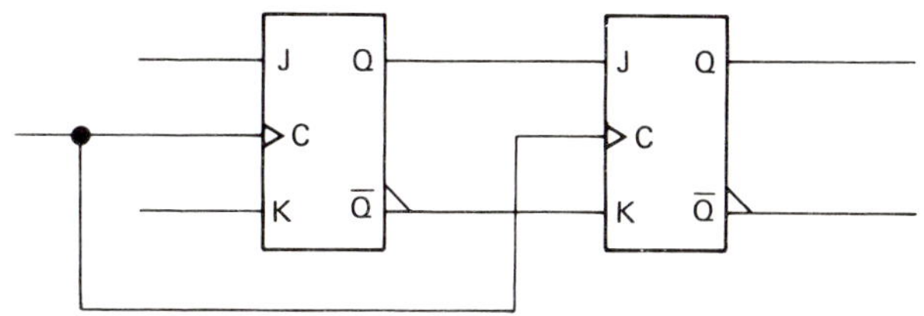

Figure 4.4 2 J-K flip flops cascaded together

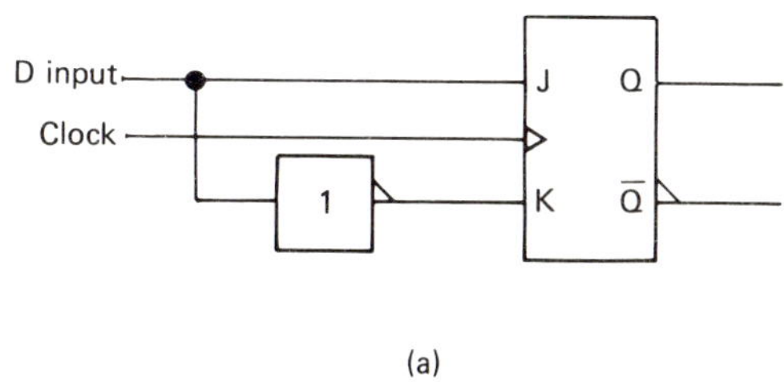

Figure 4.5 (a) D type flip flop formed using a J-K flip flop. (b) Old style format for representation of D type. (c) New style format for representation of D type

Explanation of new logic symbol

The S and R inputs have triangles which mean that they are active low, i.e. a 0 on S will cause S to be activated, i.e. the flip flop will be set.

Note that $\bar{Q}$ has a triangle on its output. This again shows that it is active low.

INPUTS				*OUTPUTS*	
SET (S)	RESET (R)	CLOCK (C)	D	Qn	$\overline{Qn}$
0	1	X	X	1	0
1	0	X	X	0	1
0	0	X	X	1	1
1	1	↑	1	1	0
1	1	↑	0	0	1
1	1	0	X	Qn−1	$\overline{Qn-1}$

Table 4.3 Truth table for a D type flip flop

Note:
X means "don't care"—the output is not dependent upon this input.
↑ represents the rising edge of a clock.

As can be seen from Table 4.3, a low on the S input causes Q to go high immediately and a low on the R input causes Q to go low immediately. If both S and R are low, the flip flop does not know what to do and Qn and $\bar{Q}$n can be either high or low.

J-K flip flops may also have S and R inputs which operate in the same way.

The J-K flip flop is made in TTL (7476) and its pinout is shown in Figure 4.6.

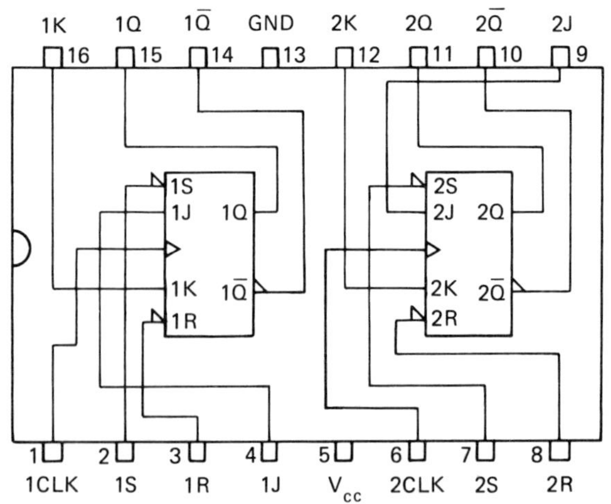

Figure 4.6 Pinout of J-K flip flop (7476)

Note:

The power (Vcc) and ground pins are not on pins 8 and 16.

Figure 4.7 shows a circuit which will demonstrate how the J-K flip flop works.

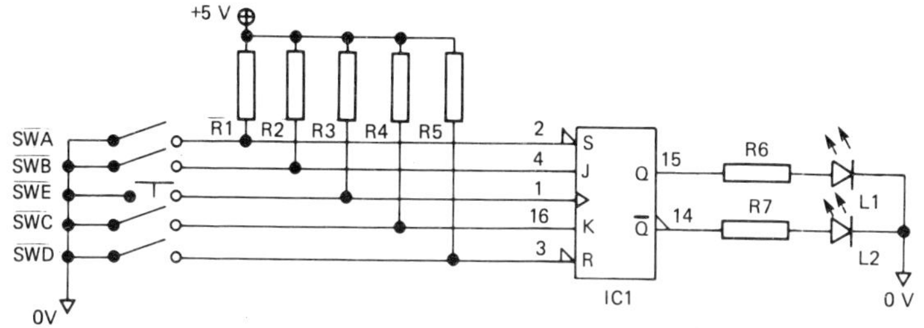

Figure 4.7 Circuit to demonstrate the use of a J-K flip flop

IC1	7476
SWA—SWD	SPST (single pole, single throw) switches
SWE	Momentary action SPST
R1—R7	4.7k ohm resistors
L1—L2	Leds

Exercise

Build the circuit in Figure 4.7 and prove that it works as it should.

The D type flip flop is also made in TTL (7474) and its pinout is shown in Figure 4.8.

Exercise

Build a similar circuit to the one in Figure 4.7 for the D type flip flop and prove that it works as it should.

4.4 SHIFT REGISTERS

It is often useful to store several bits of data. One way that this may be done is to load the bits into a register. This register may simply be an array of flip flops. Occasionally it is necessary to shift these bits along the flip flops. This requires a device called a shift register. A 4 bit shift register is shown in Figure 4.9 and the progress of data through it is shown in Table 4.4. Its circuit symbol is shown in Figure 4.11.

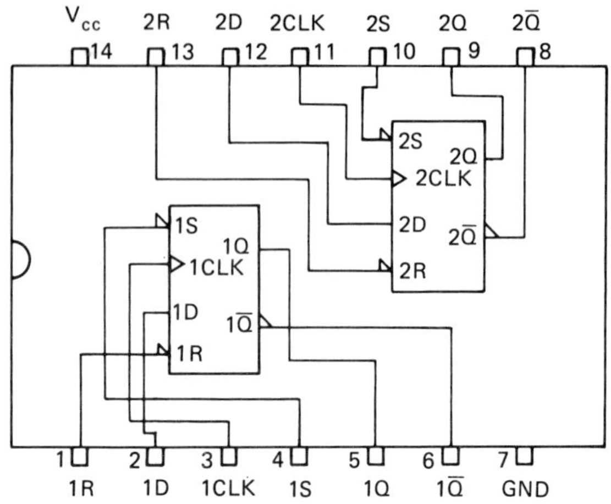

Figure 4.8 Pinout of D type flip flop (7474)

Note:

With more complex devices, there are many ways of representing them in a circuit. It does not matter how you represent a device, as long as:

1. it is clear what the device is.
2. it is clear what the function is.
3. it is easy to implement in a circuit diagram (e.g. all data lines close together, etc.).

The way that I have shown is the recommended fashion. In brief, the various symbols mean:

1. The top box is the control box. (The control box may be on the top or bottom.)
2. R is the active low reset.
3. C is the positive triggered clock input.
4. A is the serial input.
5. Q1 to Q4 are the outputs.

Appendix D explains the rationale behind the various symbols for all gates.

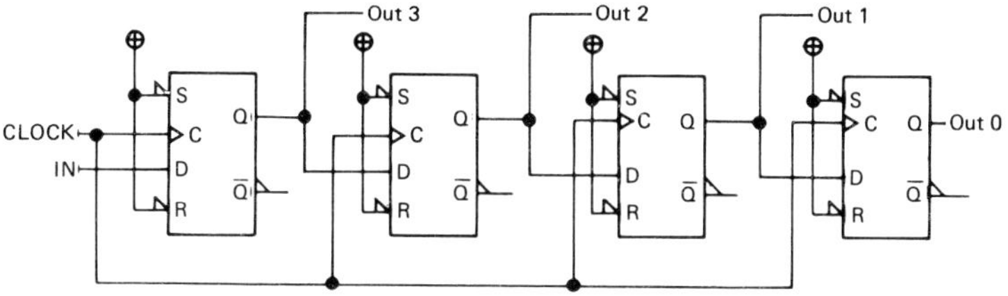

Figure 4.9 4 bit shift register

The first thing the reader should notice about Figure 4.9 is that the S and R inputs are both "tied high". Whenever a line turns into an upward T or a ⊕ , then the line is connected (or tied) to +5V. Tying unused inputs high ensures that they will not affect the operation of the circuit. THIS IS A VERY IMPORTANT RULE IN DIGITAL DESIGN—ALWAYS TIE UNUSED INPUTS HIGH OR LOW. It is often a good idea when tying an unused input high, to connect it through a resistor to +5V.

To show a connection to 0V, a line will be terminated by a upside down T or a ▽.

Another point: when a line branches to several places (as does the clock line), it is often useful to put a heavyset dot at every junction. This distinguishes branches from two lines crossing. *Note*: dots have a habit of wearing out, so NEVER have a 4 way junction—always stagger the junctions as shown below in Figure 4.10.

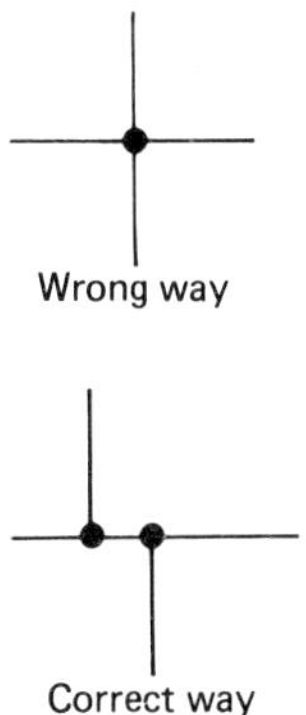

Figure 4.10 How to connect two lines together

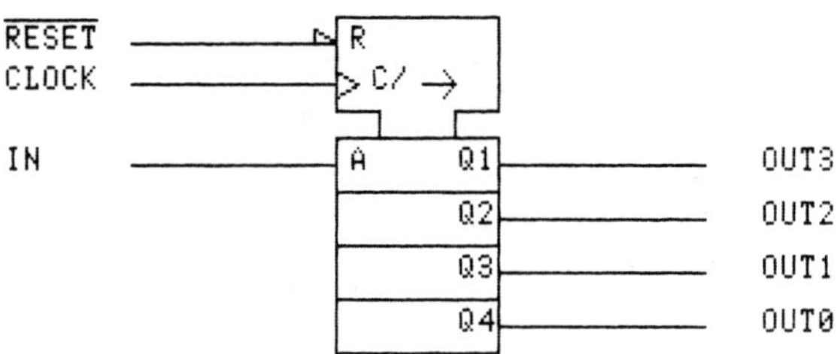

Figure 4.11 Circuit symbol for a 4 bit shift register

Explanation of new logic symbol

The box at the top is the control box and affects the rest of the symbol. Control boxes may be at the top or bottom of the main box.

The R input is an active low reset (when low, R forces Q1-Q4 to 0).

C/→ means that the clock will cause the signals to shift right (Q1 to Q2, Q2 to Q3, etc.) (C/← would move the signals in the opposite direction.)

	IN	*OUT3*	*OUT2*	*OUT1*	*OUT0*
Initial state	1	0	1	0	1
After 1st CLOCK	0	1	0	1	0
After 2nd CLOCK	1	0	1	0	1
After 3rd CLOCK	1	1	0	1	0
After 4th CLOCK	0	1	1	0	1
After 5th CLOCK	0	0	1	1	0
After 6th CLOCK	0	0	0	1	1
After 7th CLOCK	0	0	0	0	1
After 8th CLOCK	0	0	0	0	0

Table 4.4 Progress of data through a 4 bit shift register

This type of shift register is known as a Serial In, Parallel Out (SIPO) shift register. If only the last output was available, then this would be a Serial In, Serial Out (SISO). The other two types are Parallel In, Parallel Out (PIPO) and Parallel In, Serial Out (PISO). An 8 bit PISO shift register is shown in Figure 4.12 and the progress of data through it is shown in Table 4.5.

Another important rule is to have INPUTS FOR A DEVICE GOING INTO THE LEFT OF THE DEVICE, OUTPUTS COMING OUT OF THE RIGHT AND CONTROL SIGNALS IN/OUT OF THE CONTROL BOX. This aids understanding of circuit diagrams.

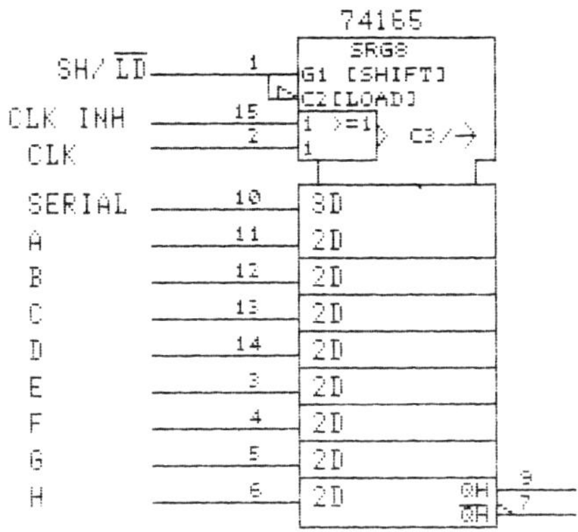

Figure 4.12 8 bit PISO shift register (74165)

Explanation of new logic symbol

SRG8 means that this is an 8 bit shift register.

The input that splits into G1 and C2 can be read as follows:

When high, the SRG is in shift mode.
When low, the SRG is in load mode.

The CLK INH and CLK signals have 1 on their inputs. This means that they are only active when control signal 1 (G1) is active, i.e. SH/$\overline{\text{LD}}$ is high. They also have ≥1 in a box with a > on the output. This means that CLK INH is ORed with CLK to produce the clock for the SRG.

The C3/→ means that the shift register will shift to the right.

The 3D on the serial input means that it is only active when control signal 3 (C3) is active, i.e. when a clock pulse comes through. This will cause the serial input to be shifted into QA.

The 2D on the other inputs means that they are only active when control signal 2 (C2) is active, i.e. when SH/$\overline{\text{LD}}$ is low.

CLOCK	*LOAD*	*INA*	*INB*	*INC*	*IND*	*INE*	*INF*	*ING*	*INH*	*QH*
X	1	a	b	c	d	e	f	g	h	h
↑	0	0	a	b	c	d	e	f	g	h
↑	0	0	0	a	b	c	d	e	f	g
↑	0	0	0	0	a	b	c	d	e	f
↑	0	0	0	0	0	a	b	c	d	e
↑	0	0	0	0	0	0	a	b	c	d
↑	0	0	0	0	0	0	0	a	b	c
↑	0	0	0	0	0	0	0	0	a	b
↑	0	0	0	0	0	0	0	0	0	a
↑	0	0	0	0	0	0	0	0	0	0

Table 4.5 Progress of data through an 8 bit PISO

An 8 bit SIPO is made in TTL (74164) and it is shown in Figure 4.13.

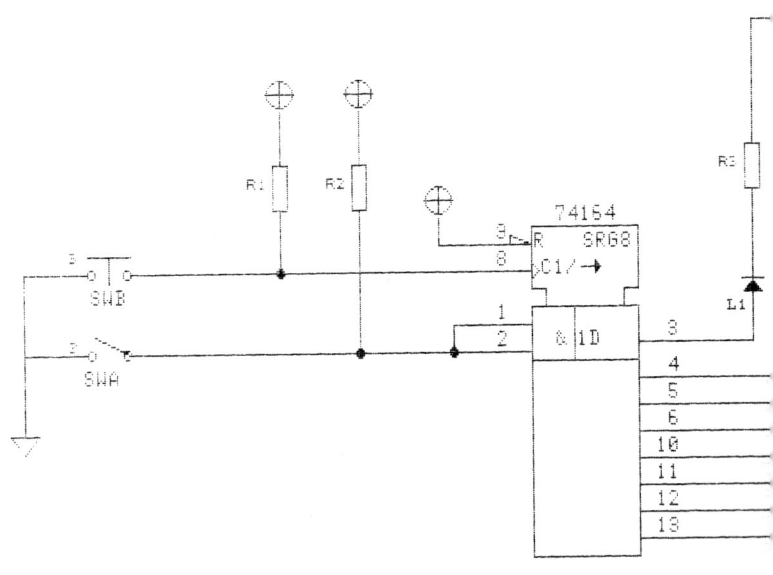

Figure 4.14 Circuit to demonstrate the use of a SIPO shift register

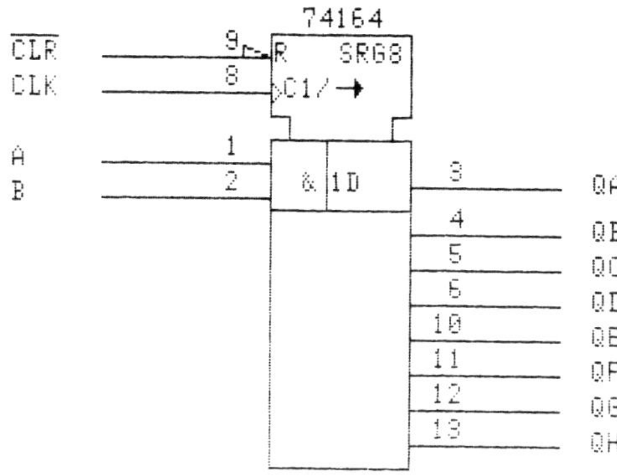

Figure 4.13 8 bit SIPO shift register (74164)

A circuit to test the SIPO is shown in Figure 4.14.

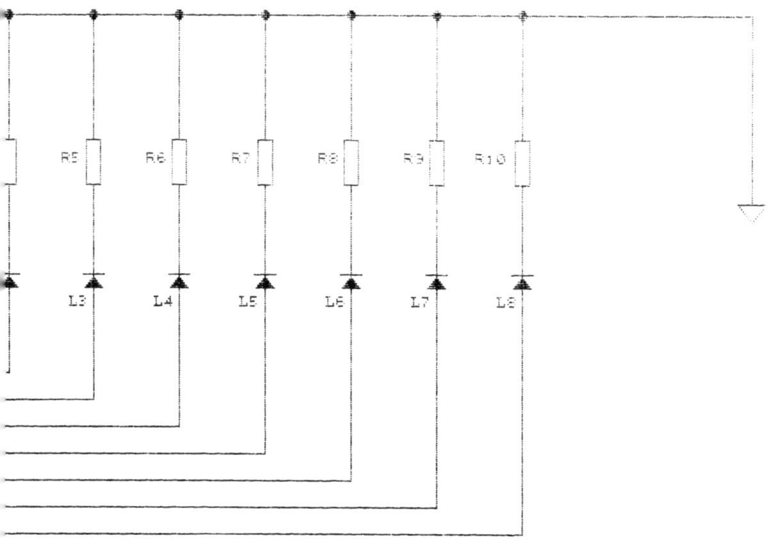

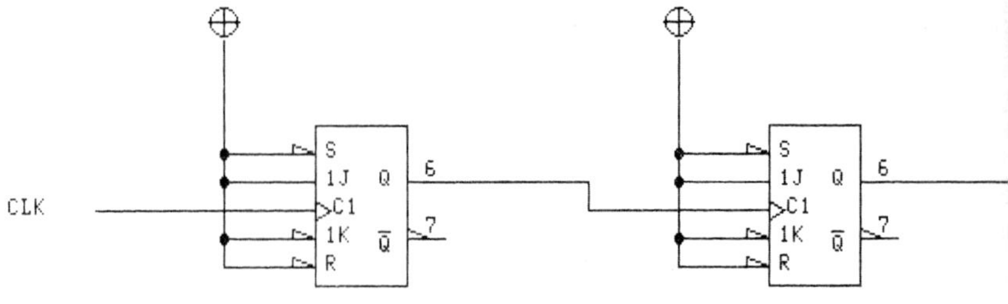

Figure 4.15 4 bit binary counter

SWA	SPST switch
SWB	Momentary action SPST
R1—R10	4.7 k ohm resistors
L1—L8	LEDs

Exercise

Build the circuit in Figure 4.14 and prove that it works as it should.

4.5 ASYNCHRONOUS COUNTERS

Counters, as their name implies, are devices which count in binary. To produce a counter, you merely cascade flip flops (normally J-K). A 4 bit counter is shown in Figure 4.15.

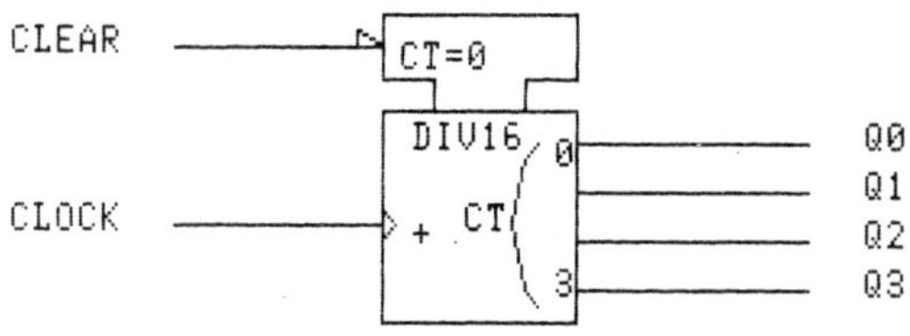

Figure 4.16 Circuit symbol for a 4 bit binary counter

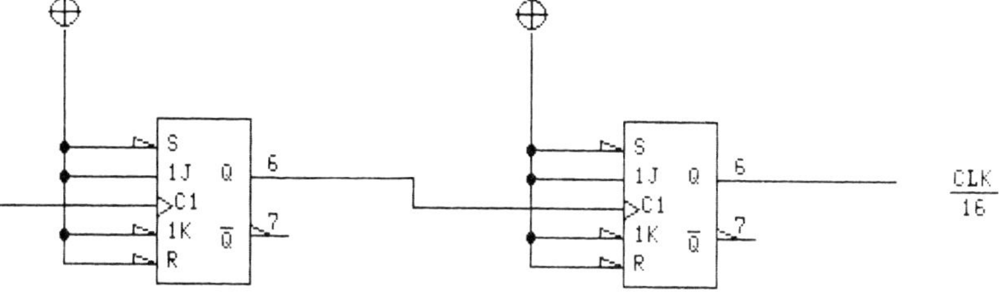

Every time each flip flop senses a rising edge on its clock input, it will change state. Table 4.6 shows the count sequence.

Count (no. of clock pulses)	*Q3*	*Q2*	*Q1*	*Q0*	*Decimal equivalent*
0	0	0	0	0	0
1	0	0	0	1	1
2	0	0	1	0	2
3	0	0	1	1	3
4	0	1	0	0	4
5	0	1	0	1	5
6	0	1	1	0	6
7	0	1	1	1	7
8	1	0	0	0	8
9	1	0	0	1	9
10	1	0	1	0	10
11	1	0	1	1	11
12	1	1	0	0	12
13	1	1	0	1	13
14	1	1	1	0	14
15	1	1	1	1	15
16	0	0	0	0	0
17	0	0	0	1	1
18	0	0	1	0	2

Table 4.6 Count sequence for a 4 bit binary counter

As can be seen from Table 4.6, the counter is cyclic. To increase the count to 32, just add another flip flop. The circuit symbol for a 4 bit binary counter is shown in Figure 4.16.

The 74293 (TTL binary counter) is shown in Figure 4.17.

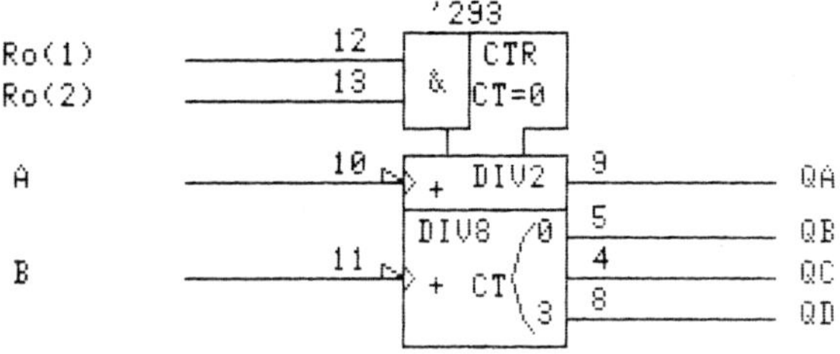

Figure 4.17 Symbol for 74293 asynchronous binary counter

Explanation of new logic symbol

CTR means that this is a counter.

CT=0 means that the counter will be reset to 0 if Ro(1) and Ro(2) are both 1 (note the & symbol).

DIV2 means that this section of the counter is ÷2.

>+ means that each clock pulse will cause the counter to increment.

DIV8 means that this section of the counter is ÷8.

$CT\begin{cases}0\\2\end{cases}$ shows the least and most significant bits of the counter.

Note that the clock input is active low.

Hence to build a ÷16 counter, it is necessary to connect QA to Input B. Ro(1) and Ro(2) are resets and will cause a reset only if both are logic 1.

The ÷16 counter will hence have Input A as its clock input and QA, QB, QC and QD as its outputs.

Exercise

Design, build and test a circuit to demonstrate the use of the 74293 as a ÷16 counter.

Not all applications of counters use binary—some counters are cyclic over a count of ten (decade counter) and other counters over counts of twelve, etc. A counter which is cyclic over a count of n is known as a modulo, or mod, n counter. Hence the counter in Figure 4.15 is a mod 16 counter.

To produce a circuit for a non binary counter, the first thing you do is to draw the count table for the counter. For a mod 5 counter, a possible count table is shown in Table 4.7.

Count	*Q2*	*Q1*	*Q0*
0	0	0	0
1	0	0	1
2	0	1	0
3	0	1	1
4	1	0	0
0	0	0	0

Table 4.7 Count table for a mod 5 counter

As seen in Table 4.7, when Q2= 1 then, on the next clock pulse, Q0 must be inhibited from changing to a 1 and Q2 must be set to 0. The circuit in Figure 4.18 shows one way in which this may be done.

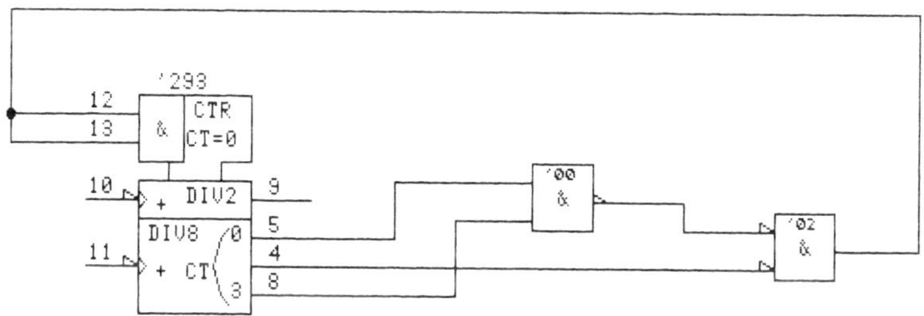

Figure 4.18 Mod 5 counter

Exercise

Draw the circuit for a mod 10 (decade) counter, build and test it.

4.6 SYNCHRONOUS COUNTERS

So far, all of the counters described have been asynchronous, i.e. the clock pulse ripples through from flip flop to flip flop. The typical propagation delay between the clock input and Q output is 25 ns. This means that for a 4 bit counter, the delay between the clock input and the final Q output is 100 ns. Hence the speed at which the counter can run is limited to 1/100 ns = 10 MHz.

Another type of counter is the synchronous counter which has a common clock input to all flip flops. This means that this counter is faster because the longest route for a signal to travel has been cut out (propagation delays are explained in Chapter 6). Figure 4.19 shows a 4 bit synchronous counter (74LS161).

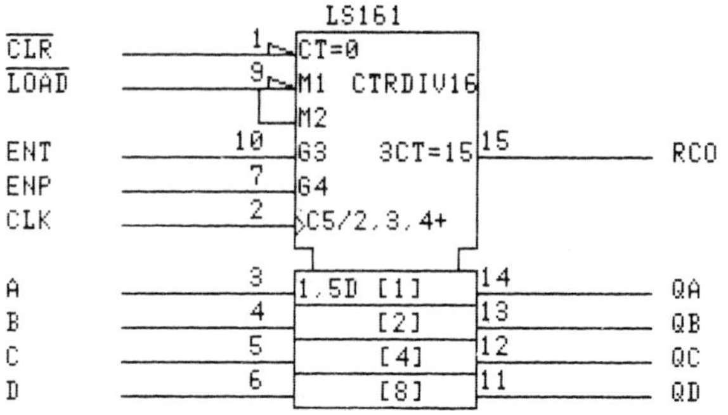

Figure 4.19 Circuit symbol for 74LS161 synchronous binary counter

Explanation of new logic symbol

CTRDIV16 means that this is a 16 state counter
CT=0 means that when the CLR input is active (low), then the counter will be reset to 0.
The LOAD input goes into M1 and M2. Hence control signal 1 is active when LOAD is low and control signal 2 is active when LOAD is high.
ENT and ENP activate control signals 3 and 4 respectively.
CLK will activate control signal 5 and will increment the counter if control signals 2, 3 and 4 are active.
1,5D means that the input will be loaded into the counter if control signals 1 and 5 are active.
[1], [2], [4] and [8] show the least and most significant bits.

4.7 CONCLUSION

The devices shown in this chapter are integral parts of many designs. The "D" type flip flop, in particular, will appear in almost every design you come across or do yourself.

4.8 SUMMARY

The devices covered in this chapter all use sequential logic, i.e. their outputs depend, in part, upon previous states. They are listed below, along with their circuit symbols.

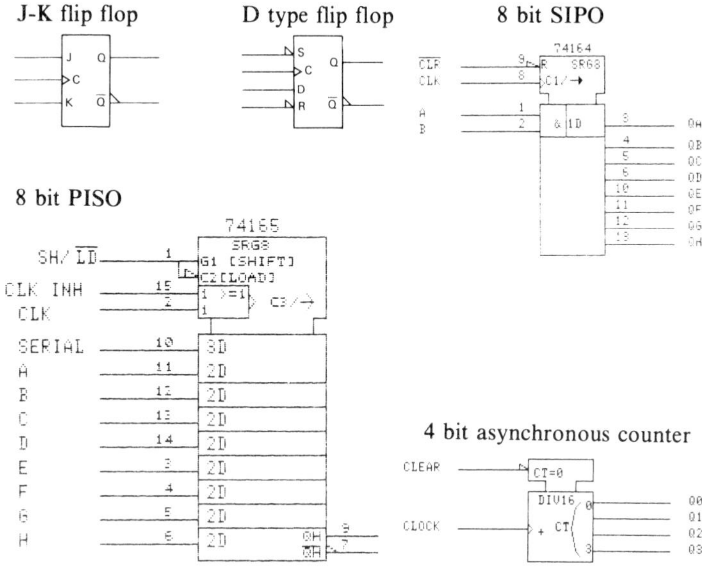

Mod 5 counter

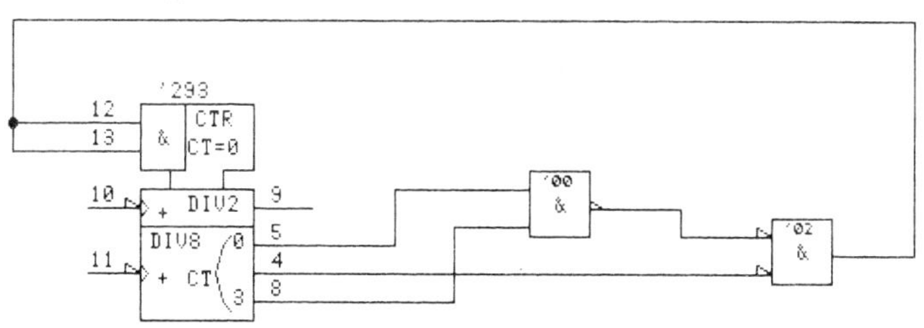

4 bit synchronous counter

5
Analog Components

This chapter discusses some of the basic analog devices available. The devices range from transistors to power supplies, and those covered in this chapter are:

Resistors
Capacitors
Diodes
Crystals
Relays
Transistors
Audible alarms
Power supplies

Analog devices may be connected together in two ways: Series and Parallel. Components connected in series have one common connection (i.e. the end of one component is connected to the beginning of another), whereas components connected in parallel have both ends connected together. Series and parallel connections are shown in Figure 5.1.

5.1 RESISTORS

A resistor is a discrete device which has the property of resisting the flow of current through it. The property of resistance is measured in ohms (Ω). Resistance is related to voltage (V) and current (I) by the equation V=IR, where V=voltage in volts (V):

I=current in amperes (A)
R=resistance in ohms (Ω)

The circuit symbols for a resistor are shown in Figure 5.2. The box symbol is the one which is approved by the BSI (British Standards Institute), although the squiggle symbol is more widely used.

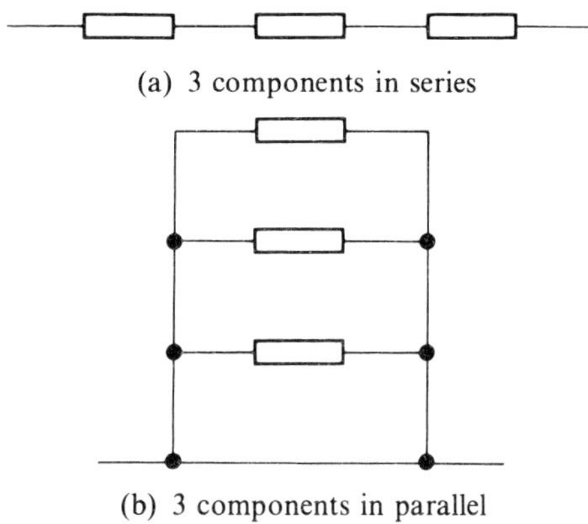

Figure 5.1 Series and parallel connections

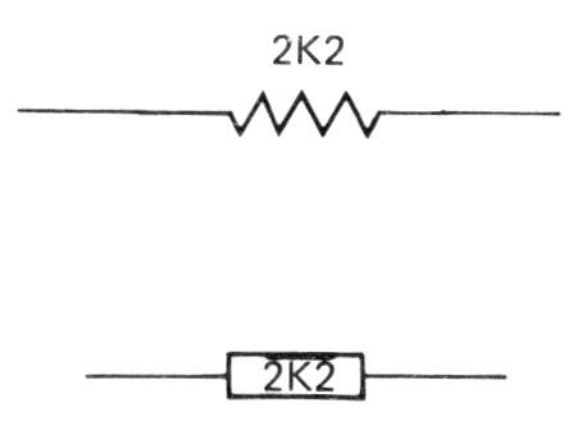

Figure 5.2 Two symbols for a resistor

The 2K2 in Figure 5.2 represents the value of the resistance (2200 ohms). Resistor values are shown as below:

Value in ohms	*Representation*
4	4R
999	999R
1000	1K0
3300	3K3
1,000,000	1M0

See Appendix E for a list of commonly used resistor values.

When you connect resistors in series, add their resistances together to get the total resistance. This is because the only route for the current is through the resistors, one after the other.

When you connect resistors in parallel, add the reciprocals of their resistances together to get the reciprocal of the total resistance. This is because the current can flow down either one resistor or the other.

Hence for two resistors with resistance R_1 and R_2,

Total resistance in series $= R_1 + R_2$
Total resistance in parallel $= 1/(1/R_1 + 1/R_2)$

In digital design, the main uses for resistors are:

1. Limiting the current through a device.
2. Ensuring that a particular line is either high or low.
3. Altering voltage levels.
4. Series damping (e.g. for MOS memory circuits).

Example

Wired OR application

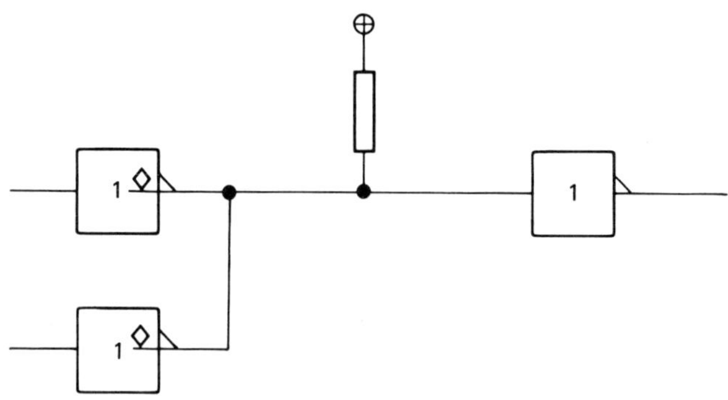

Figure 5.3 Wired OR application

The gates must all have open collector outputs. An open collector gate must ALWAYS have its output tied to +5V via a resistor.

One advantage of open collector gates is that they may be connected together in a wired OR configuration.

Open collector outputs are denoted by the diamond shape with a line underneath.

Example

External input application.

If the external input is not connected then the resistor ensures that the input to the NOT gate is logic 1. If the resistor pull-up was not present, then the input to the NOT gate would "float" i.e. it could be either logic 0 or logic 1.

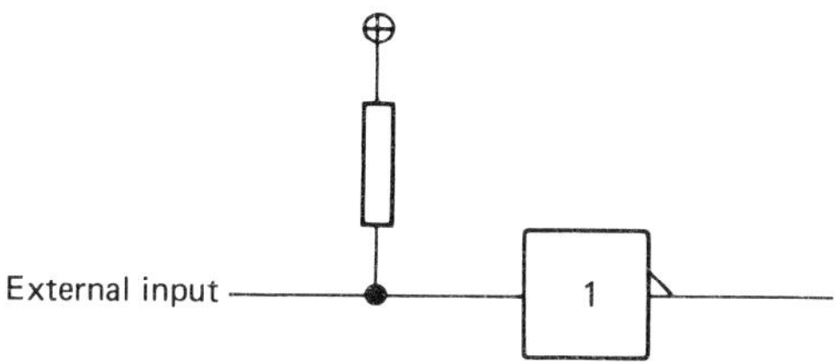

Figure 5.4 External input application

Example

Every MOS memory IC has a capacitance of approximately 7 pF per line. When a lot of these ICs are connected together, then the total capacitance becomes substantial enough to significantly slow the operation of the circuit. This problem can be alleviated by putting a resistor in series with every line. For a description of why this happens, read a book on transmission line theory

Variable resistors exist—they have a range of resistance which may be altered by a mechanical method e.g. a shunt. The circuit symbol for a variable resistor is shown in Figure 5.5.

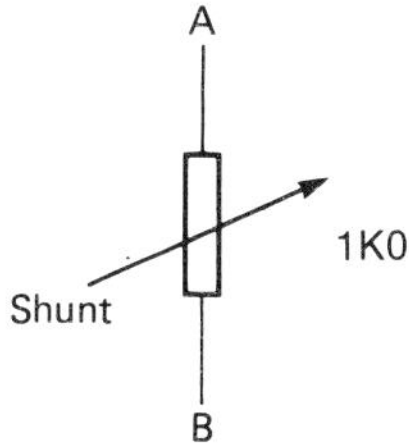

Figure 5.5 Circuit symbol for a variable resistor

The resistance between A and B may be varied by moving the shunt. At one end of the range, the resistance will be 1K0 and at the other end it will be 0R.

Another form of variable resistor is the potentiometer, which is used for producing a variable voltage. Its circuit symbol is shown in Figure 5.6.

If A was connected to +5V and B was connected to 0V, then the output at C could range from 0V to +5V; the voltage depending on the position of the shunt.

For more details on how resistors may be used in digital circuits, the reader will need to look at some elementary electronics books.

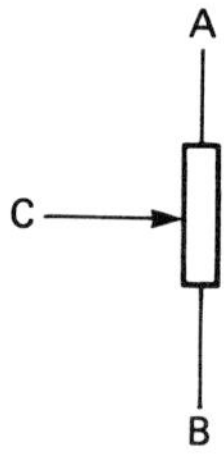

Figure 5.6 Circuit symbol for a potentiometer

5.2 CAPACITORS

A capacitor is a discrete device which has the property of resisting any change of voltage across it. This property of capacitors is measured in farads (F). A capacitor of 1F is very large—most capacitors used in digital design are in the range 10 pF to 220 μF. The capacitor resists the change of voltage by storing electric charge.

There are four major types of capacitors used in digital design:

Electrolytic
Tantalum
Ceramic
Polyester

The electrolytic and tantalum capacitors are polarised, i.e. it matters which way they are connected (THE POSITIVE END OF THE CAPACITOR, CALLED THE ANODE, MUST BE CONNECTED TO THE MORE POSITIVE PART OF THE CIRCUIT). Ceramic and polyester capacitors are not polarised and hence do not have a positive or negative end.

Note: If a polarised capacitor is connected the wrong way around, it will explode.

The circuit symbols for capacitors are shown in Figure 5.7.

The + sign on electrolytic capacitors is not always present in circuit diagrams. All that is necessary is the white box and the black box to distinguish between the anode (positive end) and cathode (negative end).

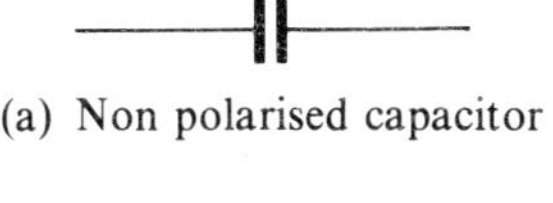

(a) Non polarised capacitor

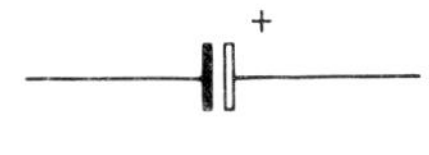

(b) Polarised capacitor

Figure 5.7 Circuit symbols for capacitors

Capacitors are mainly used in digital design to smooth the power supply and voltage rails (if a spike on the mains occurs, the capacitor will dampen it.) Normally a circuit will have an electrolytic capacitor of about 100 μF next to the power supply and non polarised capacitors of about 0.1 μF by the ICs. Normally one capacitor will do for 4 ICs.

The range of values for the different types of capacitors is:

Electrolytic	100 nF—10 mF
Tantalum	1 μF—2 μF
Polyester	1 nF—2 μF
Ceramic	2 pF—220 nF

When connecting capacitors in series, add the reciprocals of the capacitances together to get the reciprocal of the total capacitance.

When connecting capacitors in parallel, add the capacitances together to get the total capacitance.

Note: This is the opposite way around to resistors. This is because a capacitor may be thought of as a reservoir of charge.

Capacitors come in two basic packages—axial and radial. These are shown in Figure 5.8. There is no electrical difference between the two packages—hence a 22 μF capacitor in an axial package will work in exactly the same way as a 22 μF capacitor in a radial package.

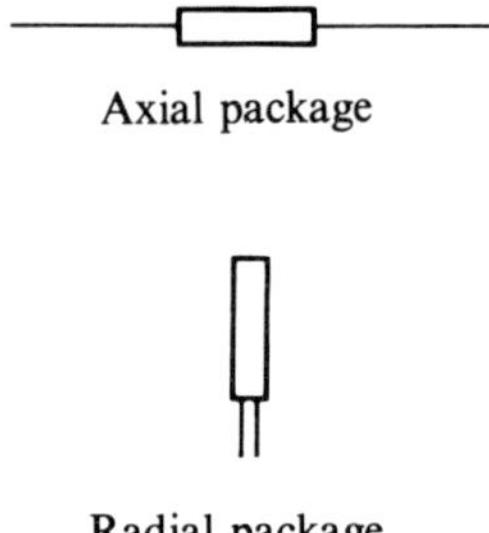

Figure 5.8 Axial and radial packages

5.3 DIODES

A diode is a discrete device which will only allow current to flow in one direction through it. The circuit symbol for a diode is shown in Figure 5.9.

Figure 5.9 Circuit symbol for a diode

If A is more positive than B, then current will flow through the diode. If B is more positive than A, no current will flow.

Diodes have a voltage drop associated with them. If current flows through a diode, then approximately 0.7V will be dropped across the diode.

Hence another way of looking at the diode is:

If A is more positive than B, the diode will cause B to have the voltage at A—0.7V.

If B is more positive than A, the diode is like a broken link (the ends are not connected).

Diodes are not perfect devices and hence do not work exactly as described. However, for the purposes of digital design, they can be assumed to work perfectly as described above. The details of the imperfections are beyond the scope of this book, but can be found in elementary electronics books.

Diodes are mainly used in power supplies and to ensure that voltage inputs to gates are not out of the recommended ranges (e.g. less than 0V or greater than 5.5V).

Light Emitting Diodes (LEDs) have the same function as normal diodes except that they emit light when current passes through them. In general, the higher the current, the higher the intensity of the light. Too much current, however, will destroy the LED and so it is necessary to limit the current flowing through an LED by using a resistor in series with the LED, as shown in previous chapters. The circuit symbol for an LED is shown in Figure 5.10.

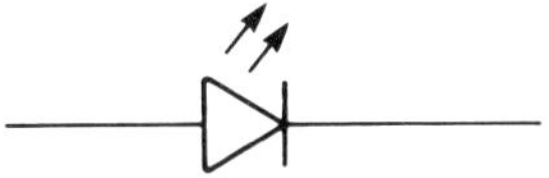

Figure 5.10 Circuit symbol for an LED

5.4 CRYSTALS

A crystal is a discrete device which will oscillate at a particular frequency. The circuit symbol is shown in Figure 5.11.

Figure 5.11 Circuit symbol of a crystal

A 16.0 MHz crystal will produce a 16.0 MHz sine wave when connected to the appropriate circuitry. Crystals are used in clock generation circuitry. A typical clock circuit is shown in Figure 5.12.

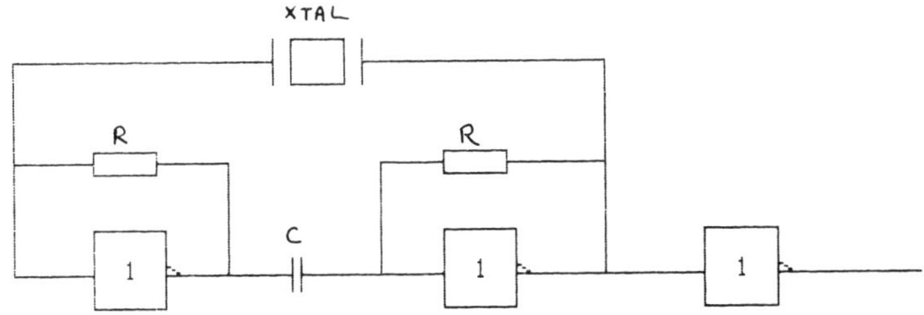

Figure 5.12 Clock circuit

The function of the circuit is explained in Appendix F. All that is necessary to know is that varying the resistor value R and the type of NOT gate (LS, S, etc.) has a profound effect upon the shape of the waveform. A typical combination of components would be:

R = 100R—3K3
C = 10 nF—47 nF
XTAL = 1 MHz—25 MHz

To produce a clock signal of a greater frequency than 25 MHz or a lesser frequency than 1 MHz, you would need a crystal oscillator hybrid circuit. These are more expensive than normal crystals but have the advantage of not needing any support circuitry—you can put their output straight into a gate.

5.5 RELAYS

A relay is a device which has two sets of connections. These connections are totally separate electrically. The relay may be considered as two separate devices:

1. Control part which looks like a resistor to the rest of the circuit.
2. Switch part which looks like an on/off switch to the rest of the circuit.

When no current flows through the control part of the relay, then the switch part is open circuited (off).

When current flows through the control part of the relay, then the switch part is short circuited (on).

The relay is very useful for isolating a signal from the main circuit. For instance, the control part of the relay might operate at 5V, while the switch part might operate at 240V.

There are other devices which operate in a similar manner (triacs, optocouplers, etc.). If the reader wishes to learn more about these, there are many electronics books on the subject.

5.6 TRANSISTORS

The transistor has a similar effect to a relay, except that the switch is an electronic one instead of a mechanical one. The npn transistor, shown in Figure 5.13, works in the following manner:

If the voltage between the base and emitter is >0.7V, then the collector and emitter are effectively connected.
If the voltage between the base and emitter is <0.7V, then the collector and emitter are open circuited.

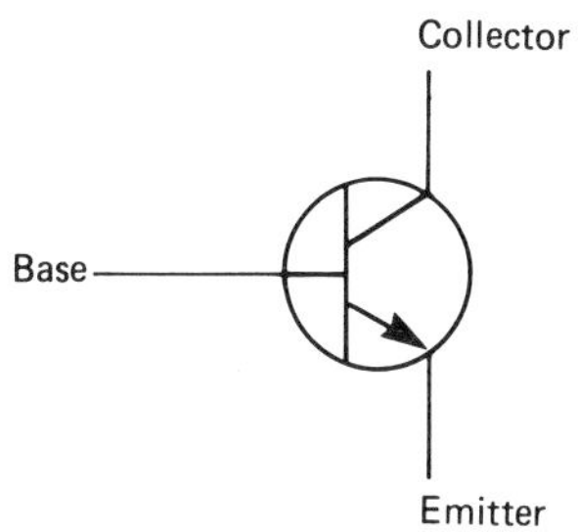

Figure 5.13 npn transistor

There are other types of transistors—pnp and FET—for a detailed explanation of these and of the npn transistor, read an elementary electronics book.

The main uses for transistors in digital design are:

Isolation of signals from the main circuit.
High current drivers (normal logic gates cannot supply much current).

5.7 AUDIBLE ALARMS

There are two major ways of producing noise from a digital circuit—one is the self-oscillating buzzer and the other is the loudspeaker.

The self-oscillating buzzer will produce a noise when a voltage is placed across its inputs. The pitch (frequency) and volume of the noise usually depend upon the voltage across the inputs.

The loudspeaker is much more simple (and hence is cheaper) than the self-oscillating buzzer. It requires an oscillating signal on its inputs to produce a noise. Different frequencies of signal produce different pitches of sound and different types of waveform (square wave, sine wave, etc.) produce different types of sound.

Figure 5.14 shows the circuit symbols for a buzzer and loudspeaker.

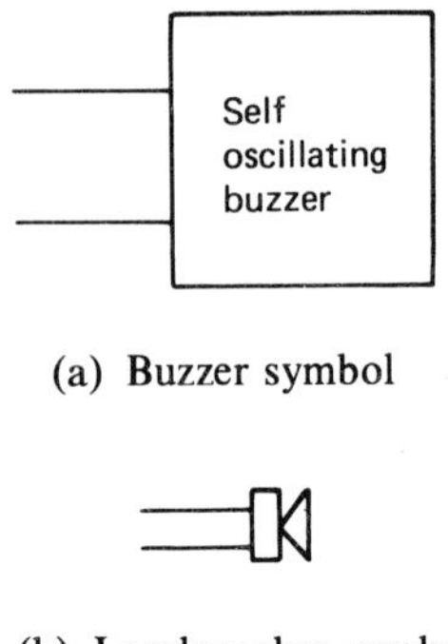

(a) Buzzer symbol

(b) Loudspeaker symbol

Figure 5.14 Circuit symbols for buzzer and loudspeaker

5.8 POWER SUPPLIES

So far, all of the experiments have been powered by batteries. Most power supplies work off the mains. The function of these power supplies is to convert 240V ac (120V in North America) to +5V dc, +12V dc, −12V dc, etc. (some digital devices need several different voltages). The dc voltage also needs to be stabilized (i.e. a surge on the mains will not affect the dc voltage). These restrictions mean that power supplies are reasonably complex. There are two main types of power supply: linear and switched mode. Linear power supplies are cheaper but less efficient (they get hotter) than switched mode power supplies.

Power supplies can be brought from various manufacturers for approximately £35.00 (for a linear supply—all that is necessary for most applications).

5.9 CONCLUSION

Analog devices are used very often when interfacing a digital design to the outside world. The reader will now be aware of the importance of analog circuitry and is advised to read elementary books on the subject.

5.10 SUMMARY

The devices covered in this chapter are:

Resistors
Variable resistors
Potentiometers
Capacitors
Diodes
LEDs
Crystals
Relays
Transistors
Buzzers
Loudspeakers
Power supplies

6 Data Books and How to Use Them

This chapter explains how to get relevant information from data sheets/books without getting bogged down by the information which is not required for a particular design. The essential data books for design engineers are also listed.

6.1 WHAT ARE DATA BOOKS?

A data book is a collection of data sheets for various components. A data sheet for a component should provide all the necessary information required to use that component in any design. Occasionally, data sheets do not contain sufficient information for obscure applications. A phone call to the manufacturer usually proves productive in these cases. A word of caution: as in other fields, it is not prudent to bother manufacturers over trivial matters which you can work out for yourself.

6.2 SOME USEFUL TERMS:

SSI Small Scale Integration. This refers to Integrated Circuit manufacturing. SSI normally has less than 12 simple logic gates (e.g. NAND gates) per I.C. An example of SSI is the 7474 Dual D type flip flop.

MSI Medium Scale Integration. MSI normally has between 12 and 100 simple logic gates per I.C. An example of MSI is the 74163 Synchronous Binary Counter.

LSI	Large Scale Integration. LSI normally has between 100 and 1000 simple logic gates per I.C. An example of LSI is the 2732 Programmable Read Only Memory.
VLSI	Very Large Scale Integration. VLSI normally has over 1000 simple logic gates per I.C. An example of VLSI is the MC68000 16 bit microprocessor.
TTL	Transistor—Transistor Logic. Logic whose gates are made up of bipolar transistors. The 74 series from Texas Instruments are all TTL.
MOS	Metal Oxide Semiconductor. Logic whose gates use Field Effect Transistors (FETs) instead of bipolar ones.
NMOS	The N and the P refer to the type of FETs used in the
PMOS	MOS logic gates. NMOS FETs are manufactured using n channel silicon and PMOS FETs using p channel silicon. The details of these technologies are beyond the scope of this book. NMOS FETs are slightly faster than PMOS FETs.
CMOS	Complementary MOS. This uses both PMOS and NMOS. The advantage of CMOS over all of the other types of transistors is that CMOS has very low power consumption.
FET	Field Effect Transistor. Devices using FETs are cheaper to make than ones using bipolar transistors. However, bipolar transistors are faster.

6.3 TTL COMPATIBLE CIRCUITS

The TTL range of integrated circuits comprises eight series of compatible product lines. These are:

54/74	Normal TTL
54LS/74LS	Low power Schottky
54S/74S	Schottky
54H/74H	High speed (no longer used)
54L/74L	Low power (no longer used)
54ALS/74ALS	Advanced low power Schottky
54AS/74AS	Advanced Schottky
74F	Fairchild Advanced Schottky.

These series are fully compatible with each other and only differ in electrical characteristics and speed of operation. Typical characteristics for SSI circuits of these product lines are shown in Table 6.1.

Series	*Propagation delay*	*Power dissipation*
54/74	10 ns	10 mW
54LS/74LS	9.5 ns	2 mW
54S/74S	3 ns	19 mW
54H/74H	6 ns	22 mW
54L/74L	33 ns	1 mW
54ALS/74ALS	4 ns	1 mW
54AS/74AS	1.5 ns	20 mW
74F	3 ns	5mW

Table 6.1 Typical characteristics of TTL SSI gates

There is another range of compatible circuits. This is the 74HCT range, which is a CMOS based range and hence has very low power dissipation.

The 54 range is for military use—the various ranges for temperature, voltage, etc. are greater than for the 74 range (commercial use). *Warning*: the 54 and 74 series are not all pin compatible.

6.4 MAIN CATEGORIES IN A DATA SHEET

The main categories are as follows:

Description
Absolute maximum ratings
DC operating conditions
AC operating conditions

6.4.1 Description

This describes the overall function of the device. It should always be read to make sure that the device in question is the right one for the design.

The description will include a pinout of the device, i.e. a diagram giving the functional name of each pin on the device. The pinouts for two devices are shown in Figure 6.1.

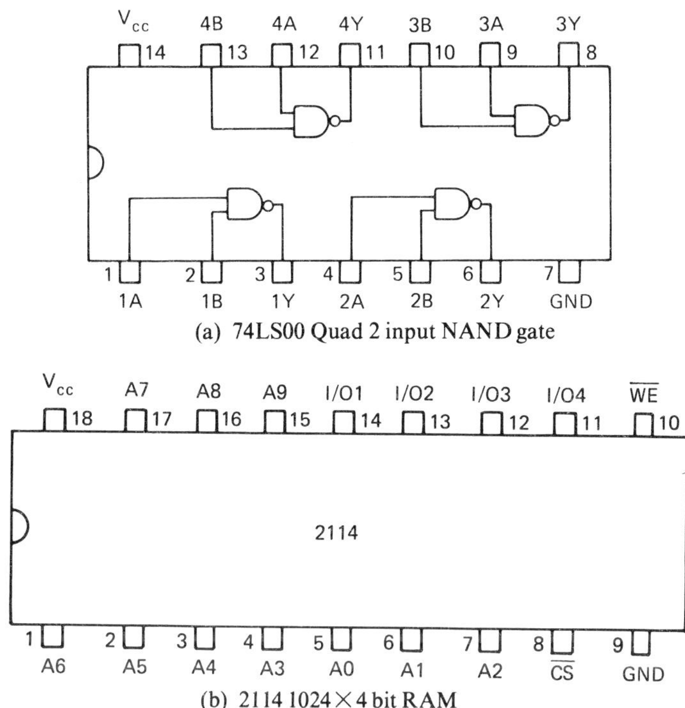

(a) 74LS00 Quad 2 input NAND gate

(b) 2114 1024×4 bit RAM

Figure 6.1 Pinouts for 74LS00 and 2114

As seen, the pinout may take several forms. The information is still the same, regardless of the format. In the second example (2114), there would be an explanation of the function of each pin.

The description will normally include a functional block diagram which shows the breakdown of the device into simple gates, etc. SSI devices often have the gates shown in the pinout diagram. LSI block diagrams break down into smaller blocks (if they broke down into gates, several pages would be needed).

Truth tables are quite common in the description. They usually clarify any uncertainty over the function of the device.

6.4.2 Absolute maximum ratings

This section gives the maximum values of things like power supply voltage, input currents, etc. It is bad design practice to push devices to their limits and so the maximum values in this section should never be exceeded.

6.4.3 DC operating conditions

This section deals with the limits of operation for voltages and currents. Two typical entries would be:

Symbol	Parameter Conditions	Limits Min	Typ	Max	Unit	Test
V_{OH}	Output High Voltage	2.4	3.4		V	V_{CC}=MIN V_{IH}=2V V_{IL}=0.8V I_{ON}=−400uA
I_{CC}	Power supply current		90	130	mA	V_{CC}=MAX

The first entry may be read as follows:

The voltage of the logic 1 outputs will be typically 3.4V (but could be as low as 2.4V) when V_{CC} is at its minimum value allowed and the input voltages and output current are as specified. This means that if you were to connect the output of this device to the input of another device which required a minimum of 3V for a logic 1 input, then your circuit may not always work. It is VERY IMPORTANT to check that this sort of error does not creep into your design. Note that S gates have high input currents and LS gates have comparatively low output currents—hence you must be careful when LS outputs drive S inputs.

The second entry may be read as follows:

The typical current drawn from the power supply by this device is 90 mA and that this figure may be up to 130 mA. If your power supply can only supply 1A then you would be taking a risk if you had more than seven such devices in your design.

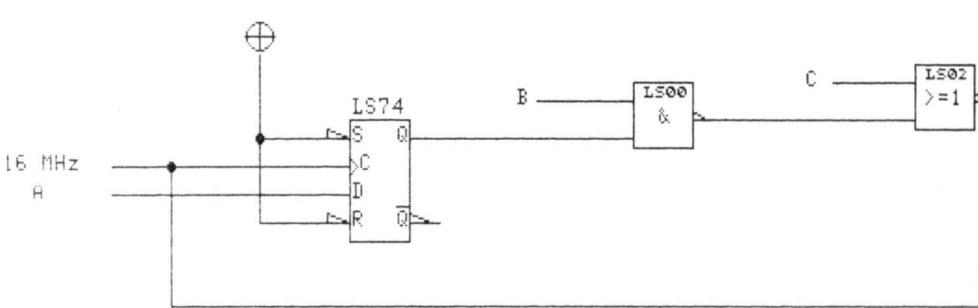

Figure 6.2 Circuit to demonstrate propagation delay

The usual parameters to be concerned with in this section are:

Output High Voltage	V_{OH}
Output Low Voltage	V_{OL}
Input High Voltage	V_{IH}
Input Low Voltage	V_{IL}
Output High Current	I_{OH}
Output Low Current	I_{OL}
Input High Current	I_{IH}
Input Low Current	I_{IL}
Supply Current	I_{CC}

6.4.4 AC Operating Characteristics

These go hand-in-hand with a timing diagram (see Chapter 7) if the device is complex. The parameters in this section deal with maximum frequencies (or minimum clock periods) and the propagation delays of signals from particular inputs to particular outputs. (When the input of a device changes, there is a small delay before the output changes. This is known as the propagation delay. The propagation delay becomes longer as the device becomes more complex.) In some designs the propagation delay between input and output may be ignored. However it is always a good idea to work out maximum delays along a signal path. An example of how important propagation delays are is shown in Figure 6.2.

The operation of this circuit is as follows:

The signal at A will affect E on the second clock pulse. Hence if the delay through the first flip flop and the subsequent gates is more than

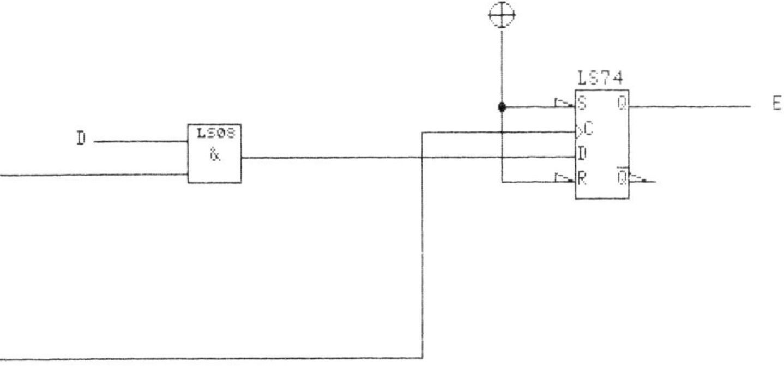

1/16 MHz = 61 ns, then there is a problem.

Looking at propagation delays in the TTL data book gives:

Maximum delay from clock input to Q output for 74LS74 is 40 ns.
Maximum delay from input to output for 74LS00 is 15 ns.
Maximum delay from input to output for 74LS32 is 22 ns.
Maximum delay from input to output for 74LS08 is 20 ns.
Setup time for D input of 74LS74 is 20 ns.

This gives a maximum propagation delay of (40+15+22+20+20)=117 ns, which is too slow.

If you use "S" devices instead of "LS", then the times become 9 ns, 5 ns, 7 ns, 7.5 ns and 3 ns respectively. This gives a total of 31.5 ns which is well under the required time. Note that the power consumption is now higher. It may be a good idea to mix LS and S devices to get minimum power consumption within the speed limit.

The setup time for a device is the minimum time that the data must be stable on an input before it can be recognized by the device (usually the minimum time before a clock pulse).

The hold time of a device output is the maximum time that data will be stable on the output after data is no longer stable on the input or after a particular clock pulse.

The hold time of a device input is the minimum time that data must be stable on the input after a relevant clock pulse.

6.5 MECHANICAL DATA

Most data books include mechanical data about the ICs. The mechanical data falls into two main categories. These are:

Ordering information
Packaging

6.5.1 Ordering information

This explains how to order the different types of ICs and their packages.

6.5.2 Packaging

There are several ways in which an IC may be packaged. The three main ways and their advantages are listed below:

Ceramic Dual In Line (DIL)	These are hermetically sealed and hence are very reliable devices.
Plastic Dual In Line	These are easier to make and hence are cheaper, although not as reliable as, Ceramic devices.
Flatpack	These are much smaller than DIL packages and hence you can fit more onto a circuit board.

For most hobbyist applications, plastic devices are sufficient. Ceramic devices would be used when a system required very high reliability. Flatpack devices would be used when space on circuit boards was an important consideration.

6.6 ESSENTIAL DATA BOOKS FOR DESIGN ENGINEERS:

Texas Instruments TTL Data Book Vol. 1
Intel Microprocessor and Peripheral Handbook
Mostek Microelectronic Data Book.

These three data books give a good set of components to design with. They are the absolute minimum requirement for a design engineer's library. It is a good idea to have as many data books as possible—several from each manufacturer, e.g. Motorola, NEC, Hitachi, Fairchild, etc.

6.7 SOME USEFUL ICs

Appendix G is a Functional Index/Selection Guide which contains most of the ICs required by an engineer to design circuits. This section gives the names of the ICs described in previous chapters and gives a typical (1985) price for each IC:

74LS000 Quad 2 input NAND gate
14 pin IC
Contains 4 NAND gates
(7400, 74S00, 74ALS00, 74AS00, 74F00 are also available)
Cost 11p.

74LS02	Quad 2 input NOR gate 14 pin IC Contains 4 NOR gates Cost 12p.
74LS04	Hex Inverter 14 pin IC Contains 6 NOT gates Cost 12p.
74LS08	Quad 2 input AND gate 14 pin IC Contains 4 AND gates Cost 14p.
74LS11	Triple 3 input AND gate 14 pin IC Contains 3 AND gates Cost 16p.
74LS32	Quad 2 input OR gate 14 pin IC Contains 4 OR gates Cost 14p.
74LS74	Dual D type with Set and Reset 14 pin IC Contains 2 D type flip flops Cost 16p.
74LS76	Dual J-K with Set and Reset 14 pin IC Contains 2 J-K flip flops Cost 20p.
74LS86	Quad 2 input XOR gate 14 pin IC Contains 4 XOR gates Cost 16p.
74LS161	Synchronous Binary Counter 16 pin IC Contains one 4 bit sync counter Cost 40p.
74LS164	8 bit SIPO shift register

14 pin IC
Contains one 8 bit SIPO
Cost 45p.

74LS165 8 bit PISO shift register
16 pin IC
Contains one 8 bit PISO
Cost 90p.

74LS266 Quad 2 input XNOR gate
14 pin IC
Contains 4 XNOR gates
Cost 50p.

74LS293 4 bit Asynchronous counter
14 pin IC
Contains one ÷2 circuit and one ÷8 circuit
Cost 50p.

There is no 74 series mod 5 counter. Other manufacturers may produce it—if not, you can easily make your own with the above building blocks.

6.8 CONCLUSION

After reading this chapter, data books should become less daunting. Some data books are badly written, but the information should still be there. It is up to you to dig it out.

7
Timing Diagrams

7.1 INTRODUCTION

Integrated circuits, as has been previously mentioned, are not perfect. When the inputs of a device change, there is a finite time before the outputs change. This time is known as the propagation delay from input to output. The propagation delays for components are included in the data sheets.

Different families of TTL (LS,S AS, etc.) have different propagation delays—this has been mentioned in Chapter 6 (Data books and how to use them). The same is true of other devices—the Z80A microprocessor is identical to the Z80 microprocessor except for improved propagation delays and a faster maximum clock frequency.

When you design a circuit, you need to check if it will work. One way to do this is to build it. This will show you if your design is valid. However, just because your circuit works once does not mean that it will work with components that are at their maximum ratings (components are made in batches within the specified limits—the characteristics of each batch may vary greatly). For instance if a circuit worked with an LS32 (abbreviation for 74LS32) whose propagation delay was 10 ns, it may not necessarily work with an LS32 whose propagation delay was 21 ns (maximum propagation delay for an LS32 is 22 ns). This is a simple example but it illustrates the basic need for some way of checking, on paper, whether your design will work in all cases. The way this is done is to draw timing diagrams.

7.2 WHAT IS A TIMING DIAGRAM?

A timing diagram is a diagram which illustrates how a circuit works by showing how one signal affects another in the circuit, usually with reference to a clock signal. Timing diagrams show the full range of timing possible with a signal. Figure 7.1 shows a simple circuit and Figure 7.2 shows the timing associated with it. Note that timing diagrams are normally drawn on graph (squared) paper.

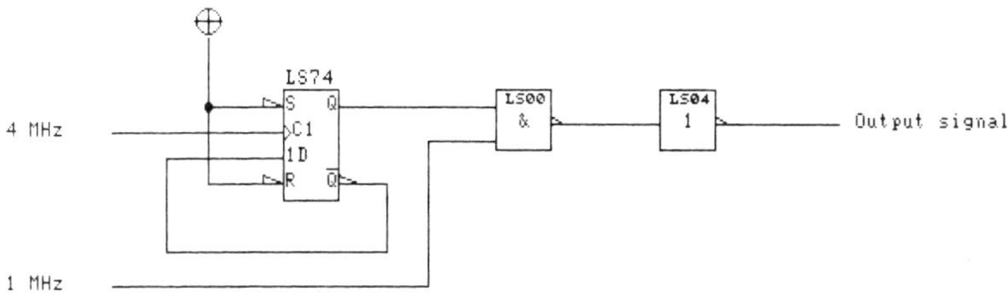

Figure 7.1 Test circuit

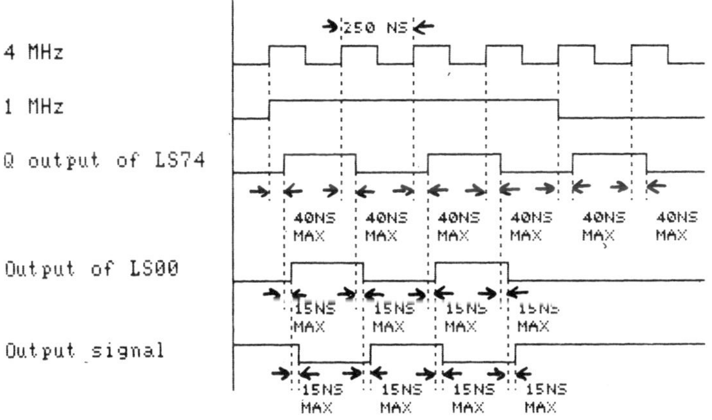

Figure 7.2 Timing diagram for test circuit

The timing diagram shows exactly how the test circuit will operate. Note that the delay caused by the wires connecting the components is ignored (i.e. the D input of the LS74 is assumed to change at exactly the same time as the $\bar{Q}$ output). This is normal practice—the delay caused by a wire of length 1 mm is approximately 10 ps and so it is not usually necessary to include the propagation delays caused by wire. Notice that the output signal can change any time from the rising edge of the 1 MHz clock to 70 ns later. Different batches of ICs will have different values within their allowed limits. IT IS VERY IMPORTANT TO ENSURE THAT YOUR CIRCUIT WILL WORK FOR

DEVICES WITH MINIMUM DELAY TIMES AS WELL AS FOR DEVICES WITH MAXIMUM DELAY TIMES. For instance, if you had a circuit which depended upon a signal not reaching a gate too soon, you might have problems.

Suppose you wanted to generate the signal OUT, shown in Figure 7.3 and you had the signals A and B. One way to do this is shown in Figure 7.4.

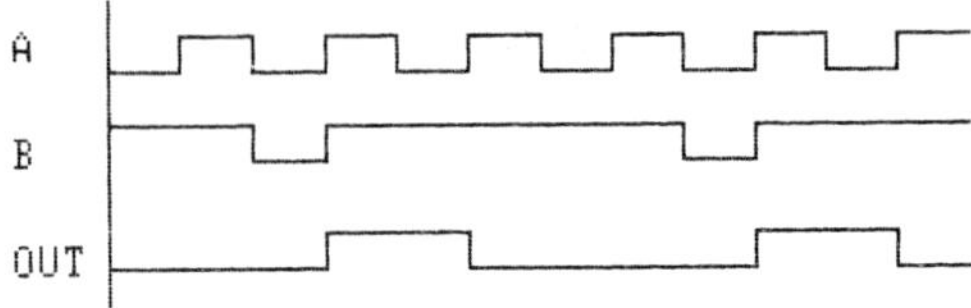

Figure 7.3 Example to show timing problems

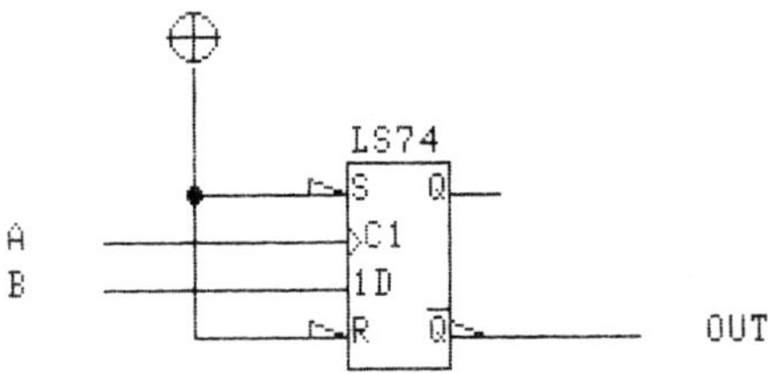

Figure 7.4 A possible solution to Figure 7.3

You have to ensure that the hold time for the LS74 is met after A goes high, otherwise B will not be latched. The timing diagram in Figure 7.3 does not give any numerical values and so you should assume the worst. Hence the circuit in Figure 7.4 may not always work. Therefore it would be a better idea to implement the circuit as shown in Figure 7.5.

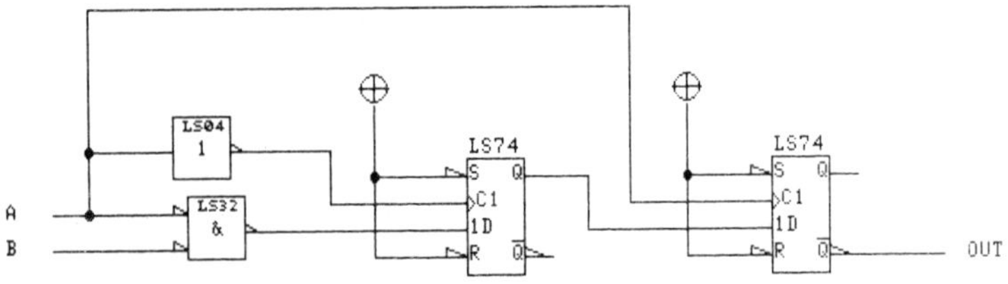

Figure 7.5 An infallible solution to Figure 7.3

The circuit shown in Figure 7.5 works thus:

When A AND B are both low, then the reset line to the first flip flop goes low, causing the Q output to go low. This is latched on the rising edge of A, causing OUT to go high. On the falling edge of A, a high is latched into the first flip flop (reset is no longer active). On the next rising edge of A, the second flip flop will latch this and cause OUT to go low. This circuit will work if the frequency of A is not great in relation to the propagation delays of the flip flops.

It is very important not to allow possible problems, as shown in Figure 7.4, to creep into your design.

7.3 PROPAGATION DELAYS

As previously mentioned, the propagation delay associated with a device is the time between input(s) changing to output(s) responding. The propagation delay is dependent upon many factors (temperature, humidity, age of the device, etc.) and may change from second to second. Propagation delays are usually given as typical and maximum values. Typical values are not really useful—if you design a circuit using typical values then the design will not always work with any batch of components, which is unacceptable in industry.

Minimum propagation delays are not usually given for TTL components. Table 7.1 gives a good rule-of-thumb list of minimum propagation delays.

Series	*Minimum Propagation Delay (ns)*
54/74	2
54LS/74LS	2
54S/74S	1
54L/74L	6
54H/74H	1.5
54ALS/74ALS	1
54AS/74AS	0.5
74F	1

Table 7.1 Rule-of-thumb minimum propagation delays for TTL

Table 7.1 is just a guide to the minimum delays—when doing a design, it is best to assume that the minimum delay in all cases is 0 ns.

7.4 SYNCHRONISM

If you have a complex circuit, doing the timing diagrams for the circuit could become extremely difficult and hence the circuit will be more difficult to prove. This problem can be alleviated by effectively splitting the complex circuit into smaller circuits, each of which have simple timing characteristics, and then mixing the smaller circuits together. An example of this is shown in Figure 7.6.

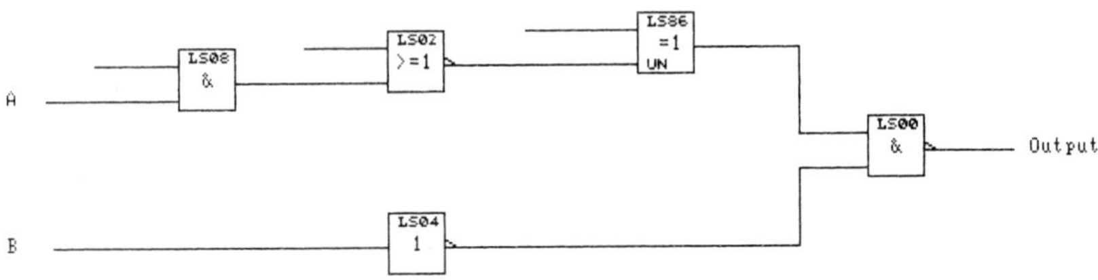

Figure 7.6 Circuit to show why synchronism is needed

The constraints on the design in Figure 7.6 are as follows:

1. The signals at A and B happen at exactly the same time.
2. The signal from A to the input of the 74LS00 must take the same time as the signal from B to the other input of the 74LS00.

Obviously constraint 2 will not be true in Figure 7.6. The signal at A can take anything up to 65 ns to reach the LS00 and the signal at B can take anything up to 15 ns to reach the LS00.

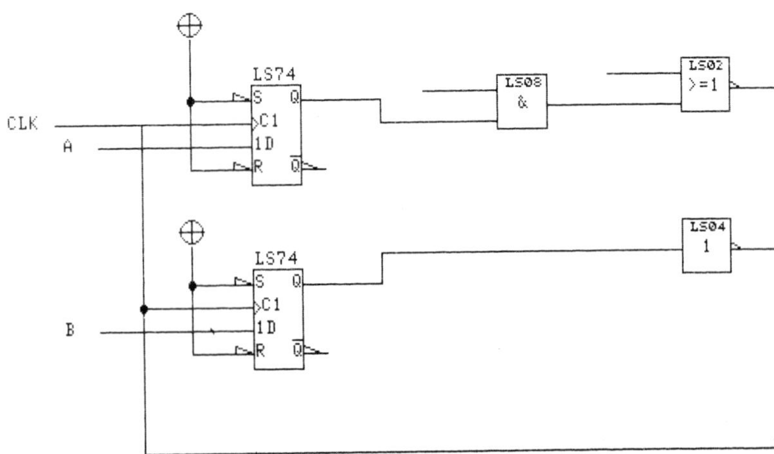

Figure 7.7 Synchronized test circuit

To ensure that constraint 2 is met, it is necessary to synchronize both path A and path B. The easiest way to do this is to use D type flip flops as shown in Figure 7.7.

The two flip flops on the left ensure that signals A and B start at the same time. The two flip flops on the right ensure that they finish at the same time (the period of CLK must be > 65 ns + prop delay across the LS74). This is known as synchronizing the two signals. This technique makes design a lot easier and increases design confidence.

This example is a very simple case; quite often circuits need to be synchronized with many clocks, of different frequencies and phases.

A clock of a particular frequency may have any number of phases. Two clocks which are of the same frequency but do not rise and fall at the same time have different phases. If one clock rises before another, then it is said to lead the second clock. Similarly the second clock is said to lag the first.

Different clock phases can be very useful in digital design. They can ensure synchronization through a circuit.

Figure 7.8 shows the different phases of 1 MHz, 2 MHz, 4 MHz and 8 MHz clocks which are based on an 8 MHz signal (phases are 125 ns apart). As can be seen, the 2M0 and 2M2 clocks are generated from the 4M0; the 2M1 and 2M3 from 4M1; 1M0 and 1M4 from 2M0; etc.

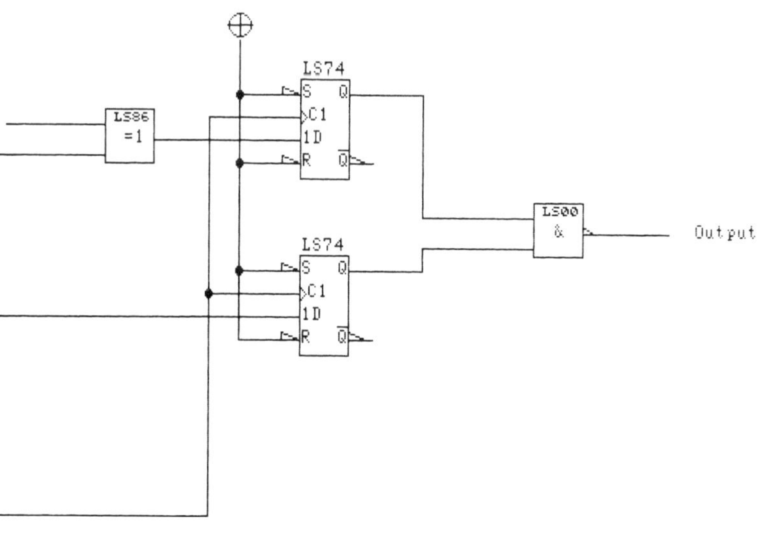

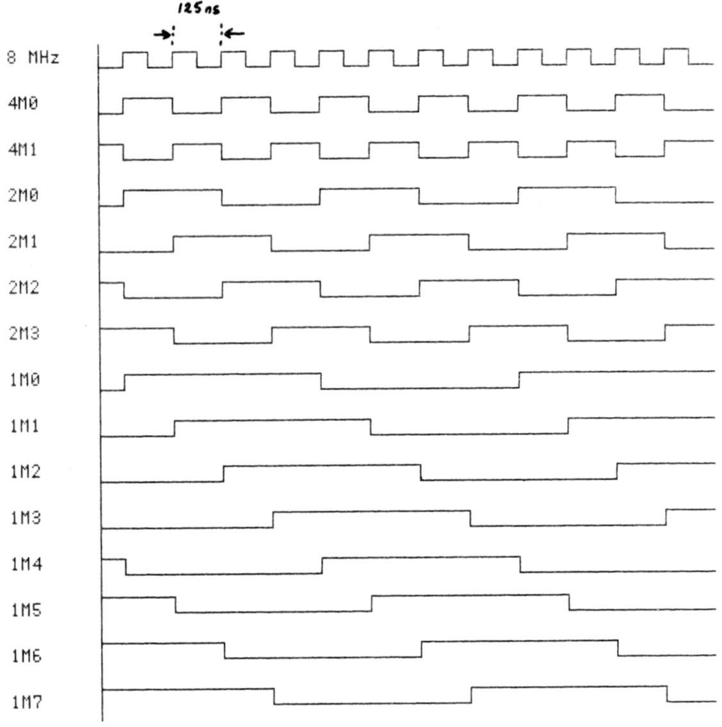

Figure 7.8 Different phases of clock, based on 8 MHz

Some circuits require many different phases—when designing, it is often useful to have Figure 7.8, or something similar, in front of you so that the relationship between the various clocks can be seen.

7.5 TIMING DIAGRAM CONVENTIONS

Figure 7.9 shows a typical timing diagram, which contains the basic conventions used in timing diagrams.

The timing diagram in Figure 7.9 can be read as follows:

The CLK signal has a period of 250 ns and is high for 125 ns.

If the START signal is high at least 20 ns before the rising edge of CLK, then A0–A15 will have a valid address a maximum of 70 ns after the rising edge of CLK. D0–D7 will be stable (valid) a maximum of 215 ns after A0–A15 is valid.

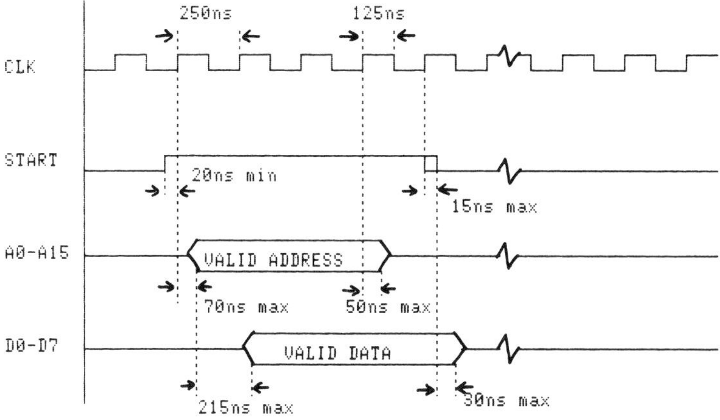

Figure 7.9 Timing diagram conventions

A0–A15 will be valid for at least 3 × 250 ns − 70 ns = 680 ns.

After A0–A15 is stable, the third rising edge of CLK will cause A0–A15 to become invalid. This can take up to a maximum of 50 ns.

The rising edge of CLK after A0–A15 has gone invalid causes START to go low. The shaded area is another way of showing that the signal can go low anytime up to 15 ns after the rising edge of CLK. After START has gone low, then D0–D7 will become invalid anything up to 30 ns later.

The break in the timing diagram (shown by ⩘) means that the signals will stay in the same state for an indefinite period (except CLK which is a continuous signal). This allows infrequent bursts of activity on the signals to be shown on one sheet of paper instead of using 7 or 8 sheets, most of which have no activity on the signal lines.

The timing diagram in Figure 7.9 is for a memory read operation. More details of this sort of operation will be discussed in Chapter 9.

7.6 CONCLUSION

This chapter is extremely important to the digital designer because timing is of paramount importance in hardware design. After reading this chapter, the reader will be aware of the sorts of problems which timing causes. Once a designer takes these problems into consideration, designs become a lot easier to do and to prove. Remember that most designs are worthless without timing diagrams.

8
Arithmetic Using Integrated Circuits

8.1 INTRODUCTION

No book on digital electronics would be complete without a description of some of the arithmetic circuits used in computer systems.

Arithmetic circuits play an important part in many designs, particularly in the design of a microprocessor. Microprocessors, as explained in Chapter 9, have instructions which use aritmetic circuits. Some of these instructions are:

ADD two numbers together.
SUBTRACT one number from another.
MULTIPLY two numbers together.
DIVIDE one number by another.

There are some ICs available which also do trigonometric operations, logarithms, etc. These ICs are discussed later on in the chapter.

For those readers who are not familiar with binary arithmetic, Section 8.2 has an explanation of what it entails.

8.2 BINARY ARITHMETIC

8.2.1 Binary addition

This is a very simple operation. There are four basic rules:

1. $0+0=0$.
2. $0+1=1$.

3. $1+0=1$.
4. $1+1=10$.

Apart from these four basic rules, the rules for binary addition are the same as for decimal addition. Hence to add two 4 bit numbers together is simple:

$$\begin{array}{r} 1010 \\ +\ 0111 \\ \hline 10001 \end{array} \qquad \begin{array}{r} 10 \\ +\ \ 7 \\ \hline 17 \end{array}$$

The decimal equivalent of the calculation is shown to the right of the binary figures. The operation would have proceeded thus:

1. $0 + 1 = 1$ with no carry.
2. $1 + 1 = 0$ with carry of 1.
3. $0 + 1 +$ carry of $1 = 0$ with carry of 1.
4. $1 + 0 +$ carry of $1 = 0$ with carry of 1.

Exercise

Add 10111010 and 01100111 together and check your answer by converting to decimal.

8.2.2 Binary subtraction

This is similar to decimal subtraction, with the following rules:

1. $0 - 0 = 0$.
2. $0 - 1 = 1$ and a borrow of 1.
3. $1 - 0 = 1$.
4. $1 - 1 = 0$.

Hence

$$\begin{array}{r} 1011 \\ -\ 0101 \\ \hline 0110 \end{array}$$

This was accomplished by:

1. $1 - 1 = 0$.
2. $1 - 0 = 1$.
3. $0 - 1 = 1$ with a borrow of 1.
4. $1 - 0 -$ borrow of $1 = 0$.

Exercise

Subtract 10111010 from 11010011 and check your answer by converting to decimal.

8.2.3 Binary multiplication

This has the following rules:

1. $0 \times 0 = 0$
2. $0 \times 1 = 0$
3. $1 \times 0 = 0$
4. $1 \times 1 = 1$

Hence

```
    1101
  × 1011
--------
    1101
   1101
  0000
 1101
--------
10001111
```

The multiplication was performed thus:

1. Is lowest bit of multiplier = 0?
   No, so add multiplicand to a register.
2. Is next bit of multiplier = 0?
   No, so shift register 1 bit and add multiplicand to it.
3. Is next bit of multiplier = 0?
   Yes, so shift register 1 bit and do not add multiplicand.
4. Is last bit of multiplier = 0?
   No, so shift register 1 bit and add multiplicand to it.

Exercise

Multiply 11001110 and 101101 together and check your answer by converting to decimal.

8.2.4 Binary division

This is done, as for decimal division, by repeated subtraction (long division). Hence:

```
         111
110 | 101101
      110
      ------
      1010
       110
      ------
       1001
        110
      ------
        011
```

Therefore 101101 ÷ 110 = 111 with remainder 11.

In decimal, 45 ÷ 6 = 7 with remainder 3.

8.3 FULL ADDERS

These are based on the simple rules of binary addition.

Suppose you want to add two 1 bit binary numbers together. The result would be a 1 bit sum and a 1 bit carry. The carry is normally denoted as C and the sum as Σ (Greek capital S—known as sigma). The truth table for our adder is shown in Table 8.1, where A and B are the inputs.

A	B	Σ	C
0	0	0	0
0	1	1	0
1	0	1	0
1	1	1	1

Table 8.2 Truth table for the 1 bit half adder

As can be seen from the truth table, $C = A.B$ and $\Sigma = A + B$. Hence this adder can be produced using 2 gates only. This is known as a half adder. The half adder works very well for adding single bit numbers together. If, however, you want to add two multibit numbers together, then a carry input is required. To illustrate this point, imagine adding two binary numbers together:

```
   1101
 + 1011
 ------
  11000
```

This addition can be split into four identical operations:

1. Add 1 + 1 with no carry gives a sum of 0 and a carry of 1.
2. Add 0 + 1 with a carry of 1 gives a sum of 0 and a carry of 1.
3. Add 1 + 0 with a carry of 1 gives a sum of 0 and a carry of 1.
4. Add 1 + 1 with a carry of 1 gives a sum of 1 and a carry of 1.

An adder with this property is known as a full adder. The truth table for the full adder is shown in Table 8.2. It is left as an exercise for the reader to produce the circuit for a 1 bit full adder.

CIN	*A*	*B*	Σ	*COUT*
0	0	0	0	0
0	0	1	1	0
0	1	0	1	0
0	1	1	0	1
1	0	0	1	0
1	0	1	0	1
1	1	0	0	1
1	1	1	1	1

Table 8.2 Truth table for the 1 bit full adder

To produce a 4 bit binary adder, all that is necessary is to cascade 4 full adders, so that the carry Out of one goes into the carry In of another. A possible, non-dependency notation, symbol for the full adder is shown in Figure 8.1. A 4 bit adder, using 4 full adders, is shown in Figure 8.2, along with the circuit symbol for the 7483 4 bit binary full adder.

The full adder is not perfect—there is a propagation delay between the inputs and the outputs. Hence the way that the carry has been implemented in the 4 bit adder could cause a problem in larger adders, since the propagation delay for the addition will be (propagation delay for a 1 bit adder) × (number of bits in the adder). The problem is overcome by using a look-ahead carry generator.

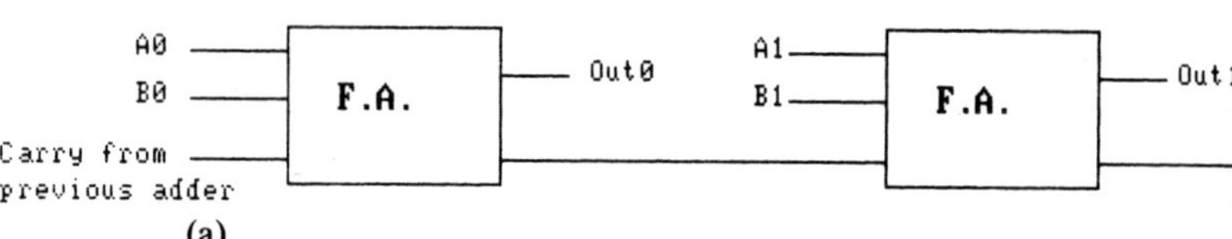

Figure 8.2 (a) 4 bit adder using 4 full adders. (b) Circuit symbol for 7483 4 bit adder

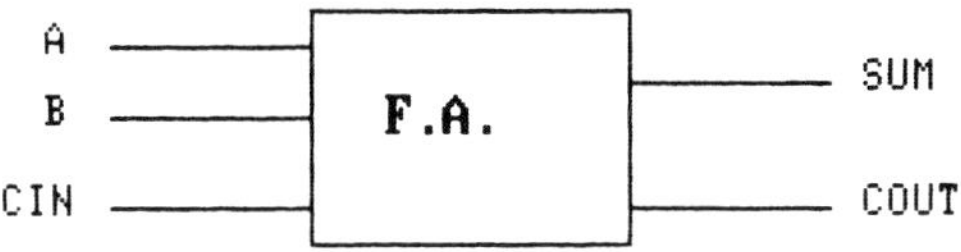

Figure 8.1 Circuit symbol for the full adder

To illustrate how a look-ahead carry generator works, we will look at the 4 bit adder:

$C_0 = P_0.Q_0$ $(C_I = 0)$
$C_1 = P_1.Q_1 + P_1.C_0 + Q_1.C_0$ i.e. $C_1 = 1$ if any two inputs = 1.
$= P_1.Q_1 + (P_1 + Q_1)C_0$
$= P_1.Q_1 + (P_1 + Q_1)P_0.Q_0$
$C_2 = P_2.Q_2 + (P_2 + Q_2)C_1$
$= P_2.Q_2 + (P_2 + Q_2)\ (P_1.Q_1 + (P_1 + Q_1)\ P_0.Q_0)$
$C_3 = P_3.Q_3 + (P_3 + Q_3)C_2$
$= P_3.Q_3 + (P_3 + Q_3)\ (P_2.Q_2 + (P_2 + Q_2)\ (P_1.Q_1 + (P_1 + Q_1)P_0.Q_0))$

etc.

(b)

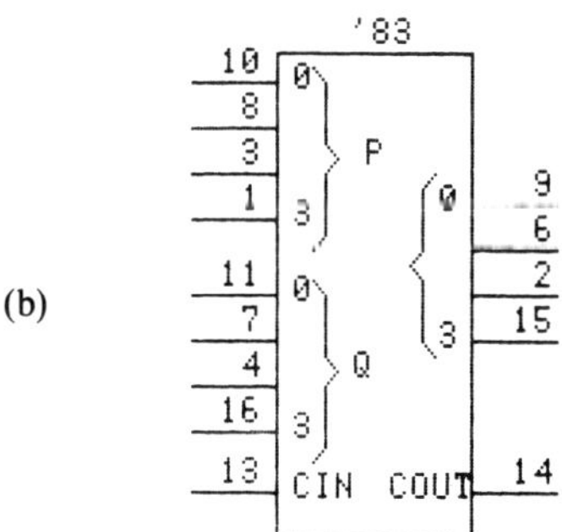

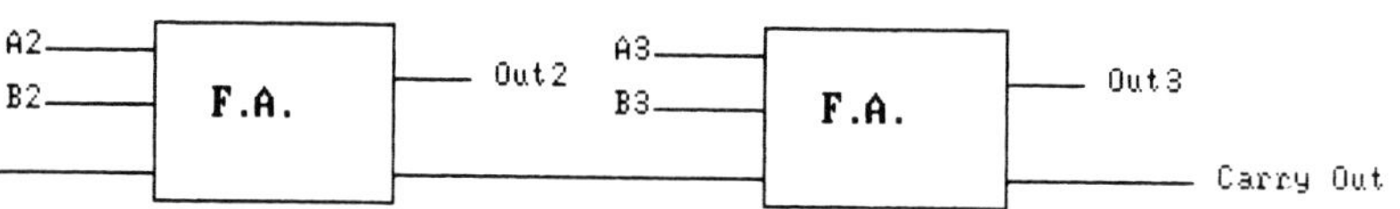

These equations may look complex, but they illustrate that every carry term can be generated directly from the basic P and Q inputs without needing to generate intermediate carry terms. Hence the propagation no longer need be limited by the ripple type of carry. A device which takes the P and Q inputs and produces the carries is known as a look-ahead carry generator.

A 3 bit look-ahead generator is made in TTL (74182) and its circuit symbol is shown in Figure 8.3. Note that the inputs are inverted and that there are 2 extra outputs—P (Propagate Carry) and G (Generate Carry). These signals are used in conjunction with the 74181 Arithmetic Logic Unit (described later) to allow several 74182s to be cascaded together.

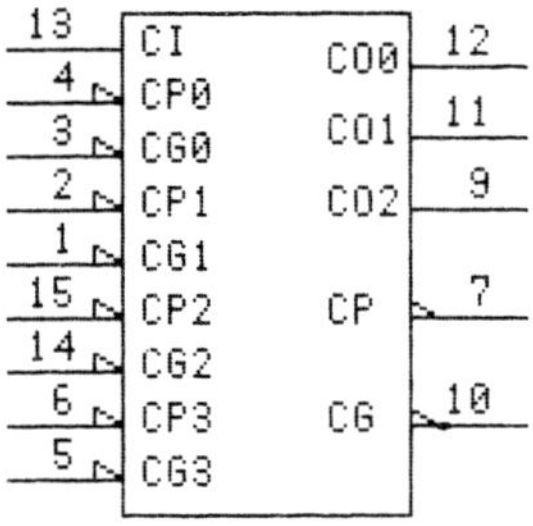

Figure 8.3 Circuit symbol for 74182 look-ahead carry generator

Subtraction may be performed with an adder, instead of building a subtractor. This is normally the method used—hence one circuit can be used for addition and subtraction. To use an adder as a subtractor, the following steps must be taken:

In the subtraction x − y:

1. Invert y, i.e. change every 1 to a 0 and vice-versa. This is known as the 1s complement of y.
2. Add 1 to the 1s complement of y. This is called the 2s complement of y.
3. Add the 2s complement of y to x.
4. Take off the most significant bit, which leaves the result.

There are special cases, but these are the four basic steps used. The theory behind this process is simple, but irrelevant to this book. Many elementary books dealing with digital techniques will contain the theory.

8.4 ARITHMETIC LOGIC UNITS (ALU)

These devices, as their name suggests, perform both arithmetic and logic functions. There is an ALU produced in TTL—the 74181. This has 16 arithmetic functions and 16 logic functions. These are listed in Table 8.3. Using 16 74S181s and 5 74S182s, it is possible to perform a 64 bit addition in 28 ns. 64 bits gives a maximum of 1.8×10^{19} with 19

M	*Arithmetic Function*		*Logic Function*
	CI=0	*CI=1*	
0	A+1	A	
1	(A+B)+1	A+B	
2	(A+$\overline{B}$)+1	A+$\overline{B}$	
3	0	−1 (2s complement)	
4	A+A$\overline{B}$+1	A+A$\overline{B}$	
5	A$\overline{B}$+(A+B)+1	A$\overline{B}$+(A+B)	
6	A−B	A−B−1	
7	A$\overline{B}$	A$\overline{B}$−1	
8	A+AB+1	A+AB	
9	A+B+1	A+B	
10	AB+(A+$\overline{B}$)+1	AB+(A+$\overline{B}$)	
11	AB	AB−1	
12	A+A+1	A+A	
13	(A+B)+A+1	(A+B)+A	
14	(A+$\overline{B}$)+A+1	(A+$\overline{B}$)+A	
15	A	A−1	
16			$\overline{A}$
17			$\overline{A+B}$
18			$\overline{A}$B
19			0
20			$\overline{AB}$
21			$\overline{B}$
22			A ⊕ B
23			A$\overline{B}$
24			$\overline{A}$+B
25			$\overline{A \oplus B}$
26			B
27			AB
28			1
29			A+$\overline{B}$
30			A+B
31			A

Table 8.3 Arithmetic and logic functions for 74181

figures of accuracy. To do this in 28 ns is quite an achievement. The circuit symbol for the 74181 is shown in Figure 8.4. The 25(P=Q) means that the function corresponding to M=25 will activate the comparison between P and Q. The function corresponding to M=25 is $\overline{P \oplus Q}$ which will be 1 if P=Q.

The (0....15) in front of CP, CG, CI and CO means that these signals are only activated when M is in the range 0—15 inclusive.

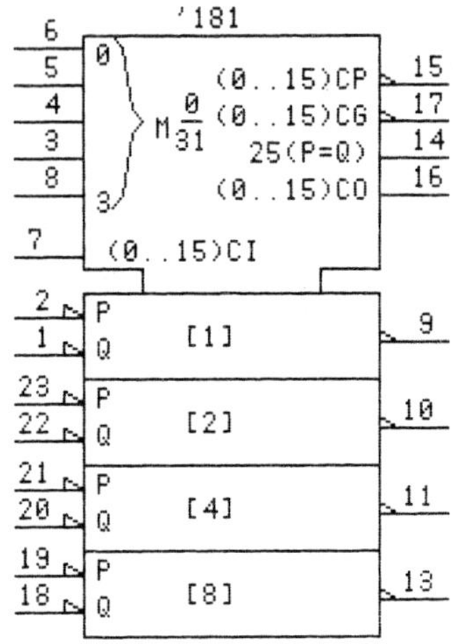

Figure 8.4 Circuit symbol for 74181

Microprocessors normally have ALUs which are more powerful than the 74181, but the principle is the same.

8.5 ARITHMETIC PROCESSING UNITS (APU)

These devices are designed to interface to a microprocessor-based system. The microprocessor will be able to read from and write to the APU via its data bus. An APU will typically include the following functions:

16–32 bit integer addition, subtraction, multiplication and division.
Floating point addition, subtraction, multiplication and division.
Trigonometric functions.
Logarithms and exponents.

An APU is normally used to speed up a microprocessor system

which uses mathematical functions (e.g. most scientific programs written for computers).

Intel produce an APU called the 8087 which can be connected to the 8086/8088 microprocessor. The 8087 can be treated as an extension of the 8086/8088 and adds 68 instructions to the 8086/8088 instruction set as well as eight 80 bit registers to the register set. The 8087 speeds up numeric processing by a factor of 100.

The 8087 has been especially designed for the 8086/8088. However, there are general purpose APUs which any microprocessor system can use. These do not speed up the operation of the system by as great a factor as the 8087, but the difference in performance is easily noted. Intel produce two general purpose APUs—the 8231 and the 8232. Many other microprocessor manufacturers produce APUs.

8.6 CONCLUSION

This chapter hopefully will have given the reader some idea of how arithmetic devices work, and also their uses. More devices could have been discussed, for instance the TTL data book has several multiplier ICs with explanations of their use, but the selection given should be sufficient. If the reader is interested in this field, there are many data books with the relevant ICs in them.

9 Microprocessors

9.1 WHAT IS A MICROPROCESSOR?

A microprocessor (μP) is the heart of a microcomputer (such as Apple™, BBC micro, IBM pc, etc.). It is usually a single LSI or VLSI chip (sometimes several chips) whose logic circuits allow it to perform certain functions associated with computers. These functions are defined by an instruction set associated with the microprocessor. Typical instructions are:

Load Accumulator with a number (the accumulator may be thought of as a shift register).
Add 5 to the contents of the Accumulator.
Store the contents of the Accumulator.

The basic operation of a microprocessor is to read data from a memory device, operate on that data and write data to a memory device (where appropriate).

The microprocessor usually consists of the Arithmetic Logic Unit (ALU) and the Control Logic Unit (CLU). The ALU deals with all of the mathematical functions (e.g. addition, multiplication, etc.) and the CLU deals with data transfers between external memory and internal registers, between internal registers, etc.

The microprocessor is known as the Central Processing Unit (CPU) of a microcomputer.

9.2 MICROPROCESSOR BLOCK DIAGRAM

A simplified block diagram is shown in Figure 9.1.

The first thing to notice about Figure 9.1 is the way the blocks are interconnected. This is a reasonably standard way of showing interconnections between blocks. It does not really matter how you draw a block diagram, as long as the diagram is clear and has the correct information in it.

The blocks shall now be described in detail:

Clock Logic

This block takes in an external square wave clock (typically 1 MHz–12 MHz) and produces all of the clocks needed in the microprocessor.

ALU

The ALU has previously been described.

Accumulator Registers

These are PIPO shift registers and are used as holding registers for arithmetic, logical and Input/Output (I/O) operations. They may be 4–32 bits long each and there may be 16 or more registers in a microprocessor.

Program Counter (PC)

This is a counter with a parallel load facility. The PC holds the address (in memory) of the next instruction to be loaded into the Instruction Register after the current instruction has finished.

Instruction Register

The Instruction Register stores the Instruction code (loaded from memory) of the next instruction to be executed.

Data Counter

The Data Counter is a register which holds the address (in memory) of data to be accessed by a particular instruction.

Stack Pointer

This is a register which holds the address (in memory) of the top of the stack.

A stack is an area of memory which is used for temporary storage of data and addresses. There are two types of stack operation: writing to

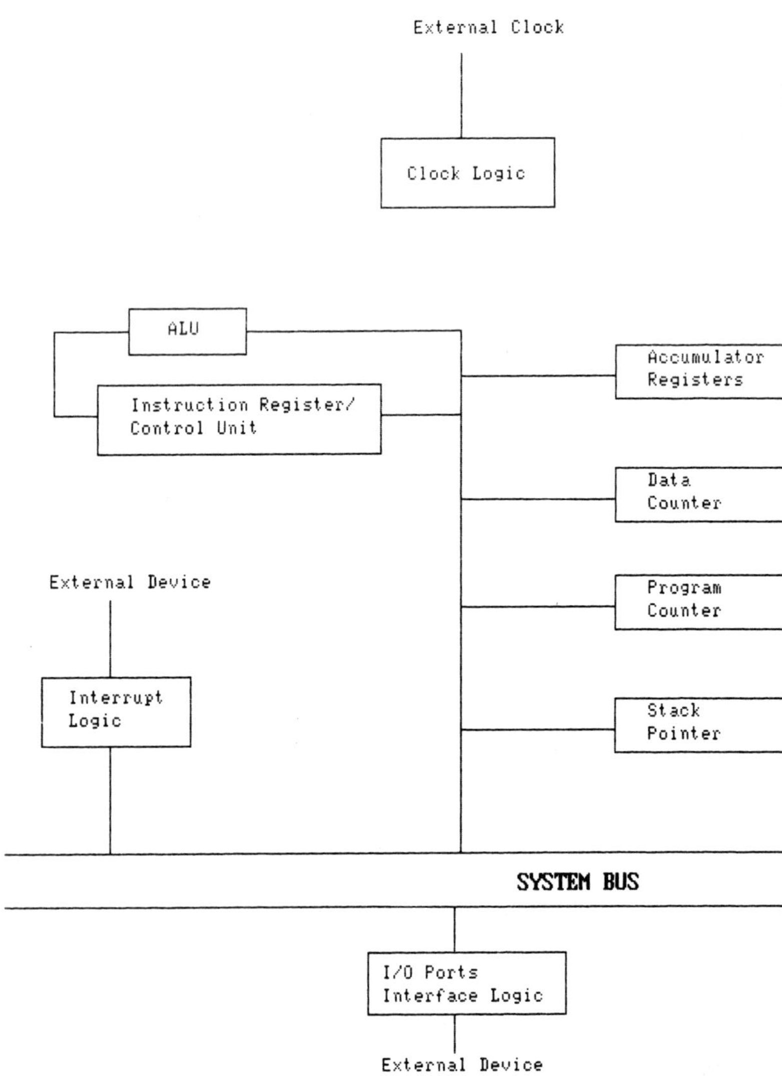

Figure 9.1 Block diagram of a microprocessor

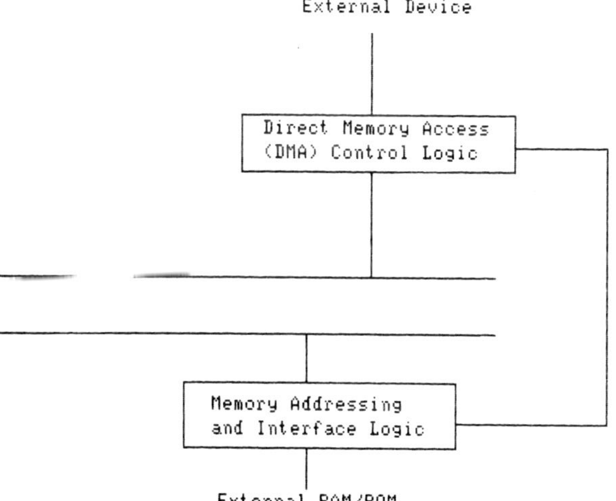
External Device
Direct Memory Access
(DMA) Control Logic
Memory Addressing
and Interface Logic
External RAM/ROM

the top of the stack (Push) and reading from the top of the stack (Pop). A stack may be likened to a Last In First Out buffer (LIFO).

Interrupt Logic

It may be necessary, from time to time, to allow an external device to "interrupt" whatever the microprocessor is doing and make it perform some function. After the function has been completed the microprocessor may continue from where it was "interrupted". The interrupt logic allows this to happen by pushing the PC and Accumulator registers onto the stack. At the end of the Interrupt routine, the PC and registers are popped off the stack.

Direct Memory Access (DMA)

Microprocessors cannot transfer large blocks of data very quickly. This can be done, however, by specialized hardware. Such transfers are sometimes necessary. To allow this, a DMA facility exists. When a "Bus Request" is received by a microprocessor it will reply with a "Bus Grant" which tells the external device that the microprocessor has yielded up its busses. When this happens, the microprocessor's address, control and data busses all go tristate (i.e. the microprocessor effectively vanishes from the circuit, leaving the busses intact). When the Bus Request becomes inactive, then the microprocessor makes the Bus Grant inactive and the microprocessor continues from where it was stopped.

Memory Addressing and Interface Logic

A microprocessor writes to memory by placing the address of the memory location on the address bus and the data to be written on the data bus. It then activates the Memory signal and the Write signal. Similarly a read is performed by placing the address of the memory location on the address bus, activating the Memory signal and the Read signal and reading the data from the data bus.

Note: Memory locations do not have to be RAM/ROM—a tristate latch may have circuitry which decodes it as a memory location. This is known as memory mapping.

I/O Ports Interface Logic

Input/Output (I/O) ports are accessed in a similar manner to memory. They act as an interface between a microcomputer system (e.g. microprocessor, RAM, ROM, etc.) and the outside world. Typically in a microcomputer system, an I/O interface IC would be connected to the address, data and control busses and would be read and written by using the I/O instructions in the microprocessor's instruction set.

The microprocessor reads and writes to the I/O ports in the same way as for memory, except that the I/O signal is activated instead of the memory signal.

Control Unit

This has been left until last because it is the heart of the microprocessor and hence the most complex.

To control a microprocessor there is an instruction set consisting of macroinstructions. These macroinstructions tell the microprocessor to perform various functions, e.g. add two numbers in two different registers. The way that the microprocessor obeys this instruction is as follows:

1. Move the contents of register A to the data bus.
2. Move the contents of the data bus to Add register 1 in the ALU.
3. Move the contents of register B to the data bus.
4. Move the contents of the data bus to Add register 2 in the ALU.
5. Activate Addition function in the ALU (Add registers 1 and 2, store the result in register 3)
6. Move the contents of Add register 3 to the data bus.
7. Move the contents of the data bus to register C.

These seven steps are known as microinstructions. Each macroinstuction has a set of microinstructions which correspond to it. The Control Unit sequences these microinstructions by outputing the appropriate sequence of control signals. The sequence of binary codes, corresponding to the control signals, is known as a microprogram. Hence one macroinstruction causes an entire microprogram to be executed.

Microprocessors have fixed microprograms and hence have a defined, static, instruction set. However there is a set of CPU building bricks with which you can define your own microprograms. These building bricks are known as bit slice logic and are defined in Chapter 13.

9.3 INSTRUCTION TIMING

All operations in a μP are controlled by an external clock signal which may simply be a crystal or a TTL compatible clock. This clock's frequency ranges from under 1 MHz to over 12 MHz (in 1985).

The execution of a microprocessor instruction comprises:

1. Instruction fetch
2. Instruction execute.

During the instruction fetch, the μP puts the contents of the PC onto the address bus and performs a read cycle. This tells external logic to put the contents of the addressed location onto the data bus. The contents of the data bus are then stored in the instruction register.

After the instruction register has been filled, the Control unit executes the appropriate microprogram. This is the instruction execute.

The instruction fetch usually takes three or four clock periods and the instruction execute takes at least one clock period.

The timing for a memory read instruction (e.g. Load Accumulator with data from memory) is shown in Figure 9.2.

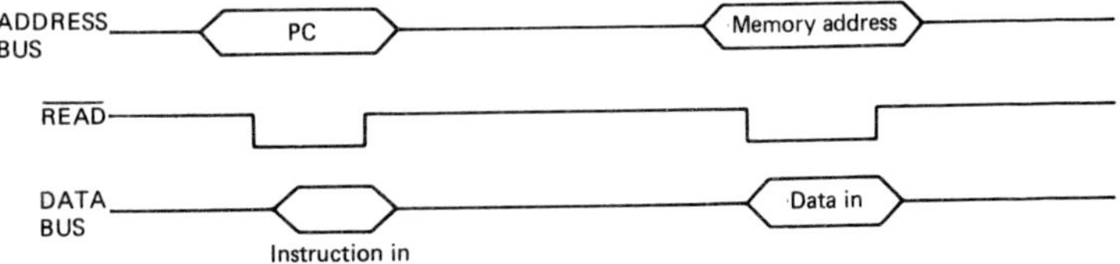

Figure 9.2 Timing for Memory Read

9.4 INSTRUCTION SET

All microprocessors have similar instruction types. These instruction types are shown below and are known collectively as an instruction set.

The instruction set may be split into nine broad ranges. These are:

Input/Output
Memory Reference
Immediate
Branch

Register
Stack
Interrupt
Status
Halt.

9.4.1 Input/Output

These instructions usually send or receive a byte of information to or from an I/O port.

9.4.2 Memory Reference

The most simple memory reference is direct addressing:

LOAD Accumulator with data at a memory location.
STORE Accumulator contents in a memory location.

Another type of memory reference is implied addressing:

LOAD Accumulator with data at the memory location addressed by a register.
STORE Accumulator contents in the memory location addressed by a register.

(Implied addressing often includes autoincrement and autodecrement features—this adds 1 or subtracts 1 to or from the register before or after the memory transfer.)

A third type of memory reference is secondary memory reference:

ADD data at a memory location to the accumulator.
SUBTRACT data at a memory location from the accumulator.
AND data at a memory location with the accumulator.
COMPARE data at a memory location with the accumulator, etc.

9.4.3 Immediate

These instructions perform operations on the accumulator(s):

ADD 5 to the accumulator
AND the accumulator with 47H.
INVERT the accumulator contents.

COMPARE the accumulator contents with 7CH (note the difference between this instruction and the one in section 9.4.2), etc.

9.4.4 Branch

These operate on the program counter:

JUMP to memory address (Load PC with address).
JUMP relative to data (Add immediate data to PC).
JUMP to subroutine (Put PC onto stack and then load PC with address).
RETURN from subroutine (Pop stack into PC), etc.

9.4.5 Register

These operate on the accumulators:

MOVE contents of accumulator A into accumulator B.
ADD contents of accumulator A to accumulator B.
SUBTRACT contents of accumulator A from accumulator B.
ROTATE contents of accumulator A, etc.

9.4.6 Stack

These operate on the stack:

PUSH a register onto the stack.
POP a register from the stack.
LOAD the Stack Pointer with data (i.e. tell the μP where the stack exists in memory), etc.

9.4.7 Interrupt

These deal with interrupts:

ENABLE interrupts
DISABLE interrupts
RETURN from interrupt

9.4.8 Status

These set or reset the four status bits in the register (Sign, Carry, Overflow and Zero):

SET sign flag
RESET zero flag, etc.

9.4.9 Halt

When this instruction is executed, the microprocessor stops and can only be restarted by an Interrupt or a Reset.

Each instruction has an 8 or 16 bit code (up to 32 bits for a 16 bit μP) which uniquely defines the function it is doing. These codes are known as Machine Code. However, writing programs in hexadecimal is very unwieldy and so a programming language for each microprocessor has been developed to aid understanding. These languages are known as Assembly languages and are comprised of mnemonics which correspond directly to machine code.

9.5 8 BIT MICROPROCESSOR

The most commonly used 8 bit microprocessors are shown in Table 9.1. All 8 bit microprocessors have an 8 bit data bus and a 16 bit address bus (which allows addressing of 64 Kbytes).

Name	*Manufacturer*
6800	Motorola
6809	Motorola
6502	Mostek
8085	Intel
Z80	Zilog

Table 9.1 Most commonly used 8 bit microprocessors

These microprocessors all have slightly different architectures. Table 9.2 compares the various features that each microprocessor has.

Feature	*6800*	*6809*	*6502*	*8085*	*Z80*
No. of addressing modes	7	10	6	7	9
Maskable interrupts	1	1	1	3	1
Non maskable interrupts	1	1	1	1	1
Internal registers	6	9	6	10	22
Maximum frequency*	2 MHz	2 MHz	3 MHz	5 MHz	8 MHz
Serial I/O port	No	No	No	Yes	No
Dynamic RAM refresh signal	No	No	No	No	Yes

Table 9.2 Comparison of 8 bit microprocessors

* Table 9.3 shows the different ICs, with approximate 1985 prices.

Explanation of Table 9.2:

No. of addressing modes: e.g. direct, implied, etc.
Maskable interrupt: an interrupt which may be disabled by the μP.
Non maskable interrupt: cannot be disabled by the μP.
Internal registers: all accumulators, stack pointers, etc.
Max frequency: how fast the microprocessor runs.
Serial I/O port: the 8085 can receive or send serial data.
Dynamic RAM refresh signal: the Z80 can refresh dynamic RAMs.

Name	*Maximum clock frequency*	*Approximate 1985 cost*
MC6800	1 MHz	£3.50
MC68A00	1.5 MHz	£4.00
MC68B00	2 MHz	£4.50
MC6809	1 MHz	£7.50
MC68A09	1.5 MHz	£14.00
MC68B09	2 MHz	£17.00
6502	1 MHz	£5.00
6502A	2 MHz	£7.00
6502B	3 MHz	£9.00
8085A	3 MHz	£2.00
8085A-2	5 MHz	£5.00
Z80 CPU	2.5 MHz	£3.00
Z80A CPU	4 MHz	£5.00
Z80B CPU	6 MHz	£9.00
Z80H CPU	8 MHz	Not available

Table 9.3 Different 8 bit μPs with approximate 1985 prices

Most new designs with 8 bit microprocessors are done with Z80s. This is because they are easy to use, cheap and very plentiful. The next section is devoted to the idiosyncracies of the Z80.

9.6 Z80 CPU

The Z80 is housed in a 40 pin IC, whose pinout is shown in Figure 9.3.

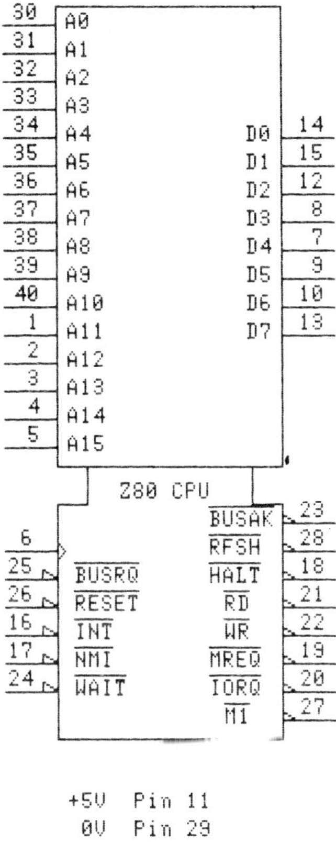

Figure 9.3 Z80 pinout/circuit symbol

The circuit symbol does not use the dependency notation because the full symbol would be unnecessarily complex for the reader.

The pins have the following functions:

A0—A15 (Tristate output) 16 bit address bus capable of addressing 65536 unique locations.

D0—D7 (Tristate input/output) 8 bit data bus for data transfer.

$\overline{\text{RFSH}}$ — (Output). When low, $\overline{\text{RFSH}}$ indicates that the lower 7 bits of the address bus contain a refresh address for dynamic RAMs (see Chapter 10).

$\overline{\text{RD}}$ — (Tristate output). When low, $\overline{\text{RD}}$ indicates that the CPU wants to read data from memory or an I/O device.

$\overline{\text{WR}}$ — (Tristate output). When low, $\overline{\text{WR}}$ indicates that the data bus has data on it to be stored in memory or I/O.

$\overline{\text{MREQ}}$ — (Tristate output). When low, $\overline{\text{MREQ}}$ indicates that the address bus has a valid memory address on it.

$\overline{\text{IORQ}}$ — (Tristate output). When low, $\overline{\text{IORQ}}$ indicates that *the lower half of the address bus* has a valid I/O address on it. $\overline{\text{IORQ}}$ is also generated with $\overline{\text{M1}}$ when an interrupt is acknowledged.

$\overline{\text{M1}}$ — (Output). When $\overline{\text{M1}}$ is low, then the Instruction fetch is in operation. $\overline{\text{M1}}$ also occurs with $\overline{\text{IORQ}}$ during an interrupt acknowledge cycle.

CLK — (Input). Clock input.

$\overline{\text{RESET}}$ — (Input, active low). When low, $\overline{\text{RESET}}$ will do the following things:

1. Set the PC to 0000
2. Disable Interrupts
3. Set register pair IR to 0000
4. Set Interrupt Mode 0.

$\overline{\text{NMI}}$ — (Input, negative edge triggered). When $\overline{\text{NMI}}$ changes from a 1 to a 0, the CPU will save the PC on the stack and jump to location 0066H in memory immediately after the current instruction is processed. $\overline{\text{NMI}}$ has a higher priority than $\overline{\text{INT}}$.

$\overline{\text{INT}}$ — (Input, active low). When $\overline{\text{INT}}$ is low and $\overline{\text{BUSRQ}}$ is high and the interrupt flag is not disabled, the CPU will accept the interrupt immediately after the present instruction has been processed. The CPU can respond to $\overline{\text{INT}}$ in 3 ways—see later.

$\overline{\text{WAIT}}$ — (Input, active low). If $\overline{\text{WAIT}}$ is low during T2 (explained later), then the CPU will insert wait states in its processing. A wait state effectively freezes the CPU processing. The $\overline{\text{WAIT}}$ signal is used to synchronize memory and I/O devices, which run at any speed, to the CPU.

$\overline{\text{BUSRQ}}$ (Input, active low). When $\overline{\text{BUSRQ}}$ goes low, the CPU will go tristate (all of the tristate inputs and outputs on the CPU will effectively disappear from the circuit) at the end of the current CPU machine cycle.

$\overline{\text{HALT}}$ (Output, active low). When low, the CPU has executed a $\overline{\text{HALT}}$ instruction and will not respond to any signal except an interrupt. While halted, the CPU executes NOPs so that the memory can be refreshed.

$\overline{\text{BUSAK}}$ (Output, active low). When low, the CPU has gone tristate. This signal will go high after $\overline{\text{BUSRQ}}$ goes high.

Note that the circuit symbol does not use the dependency notation. This is because the full symbol would be unnecessarily complex for the reader.

9.6.1 Z80 timing

The Z80 has six different types of operation. These are:

Instruction fetch
Memory read/write
I/O read/write
Interrupt request/acknowledge
Non maskable interrupt request/acknowledge
Bus request/acknowledge.

These operations take between three and six clock cycles (known as T states in this context) if no wait states are inserted. Figures 9.4 to 9.9 show the timing diagrams for these operations. Table 9.4 gives the a.c. characteristics for the various types of Z80. The reason why the full set of timing diagrams and a.c. characteristics are included is that it is very important that the reader understands exactly how the Z80 works. In addition, most Z80 timing diagrams (as for most μPs) are difficult to take in at a glance whereas, hopefully, the following

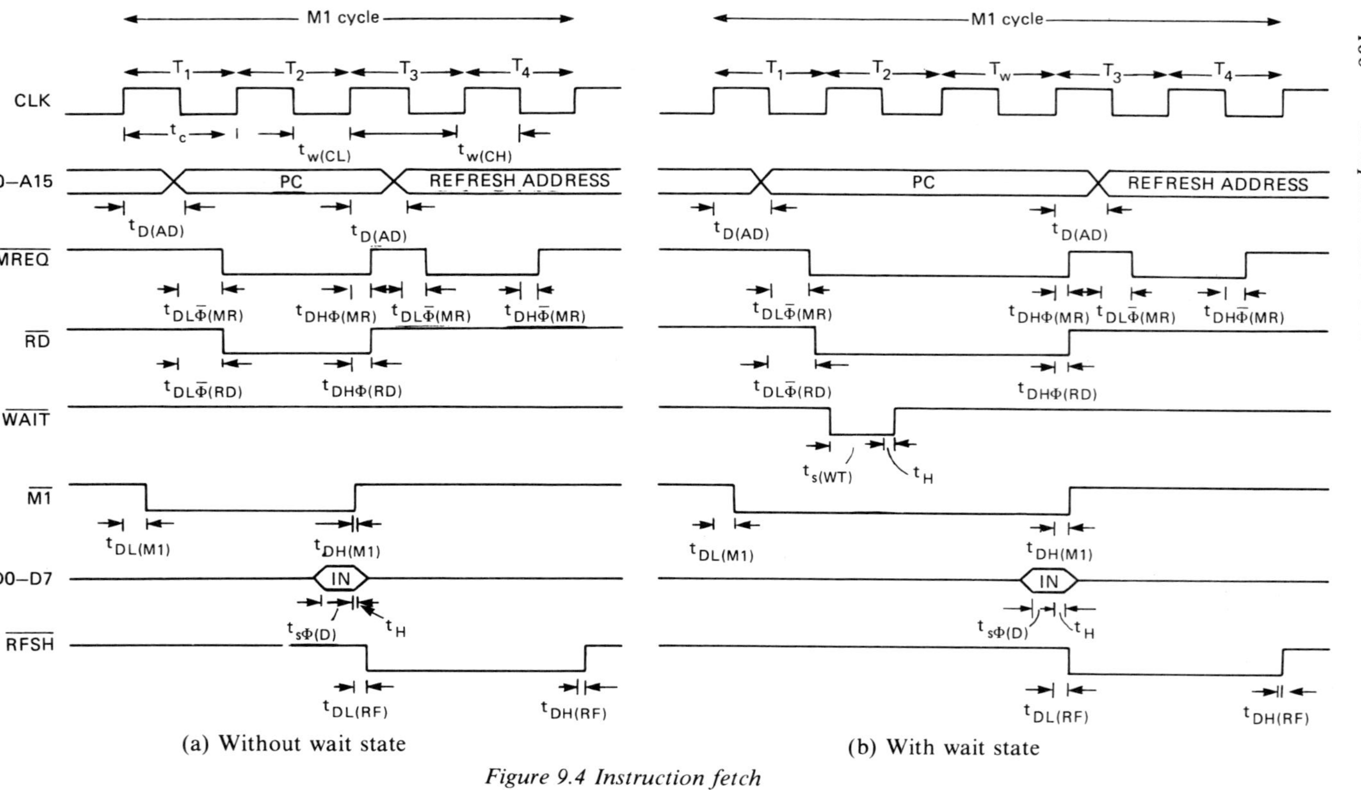

Figure 9.4 Instruction fetch

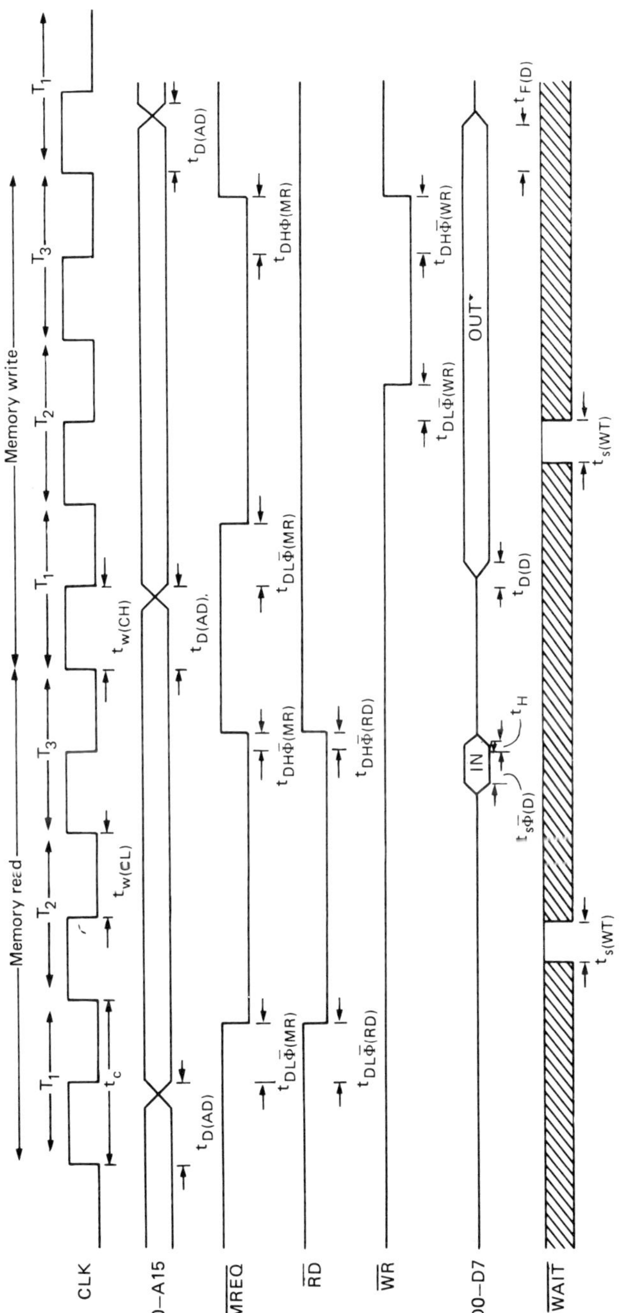

Figure 9.5 Memory Read/Write

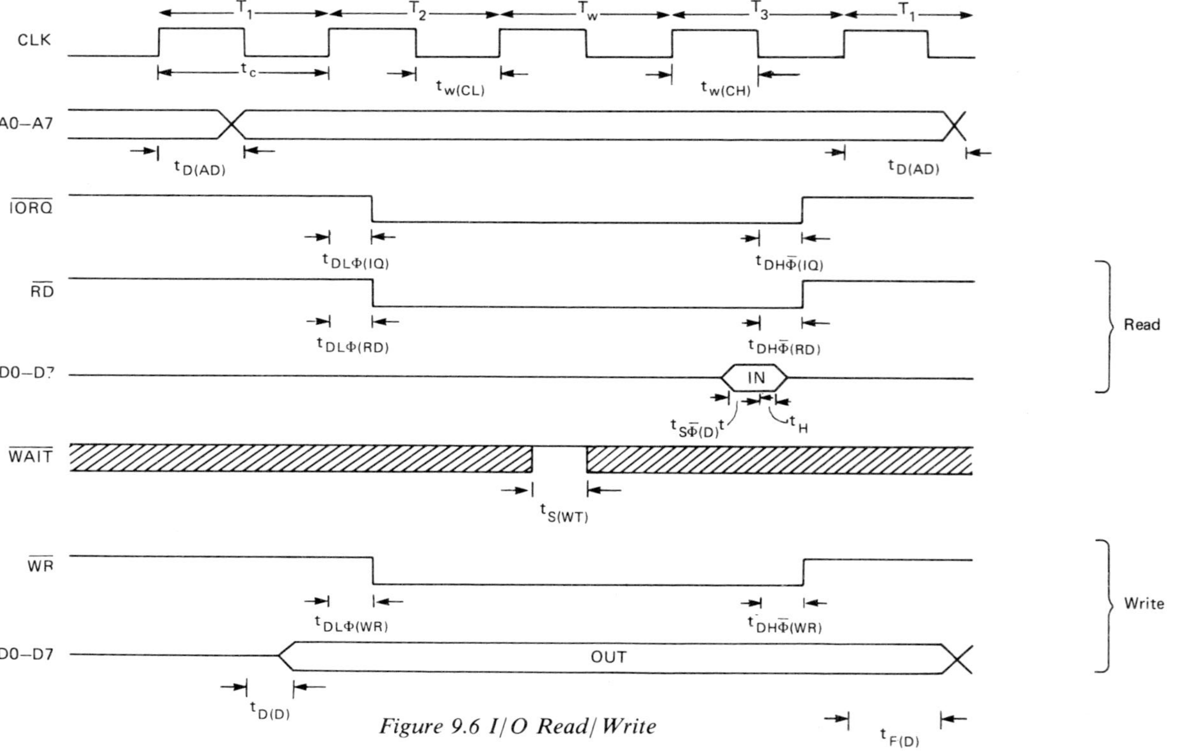

Figure 9.6 I/O Read/Write

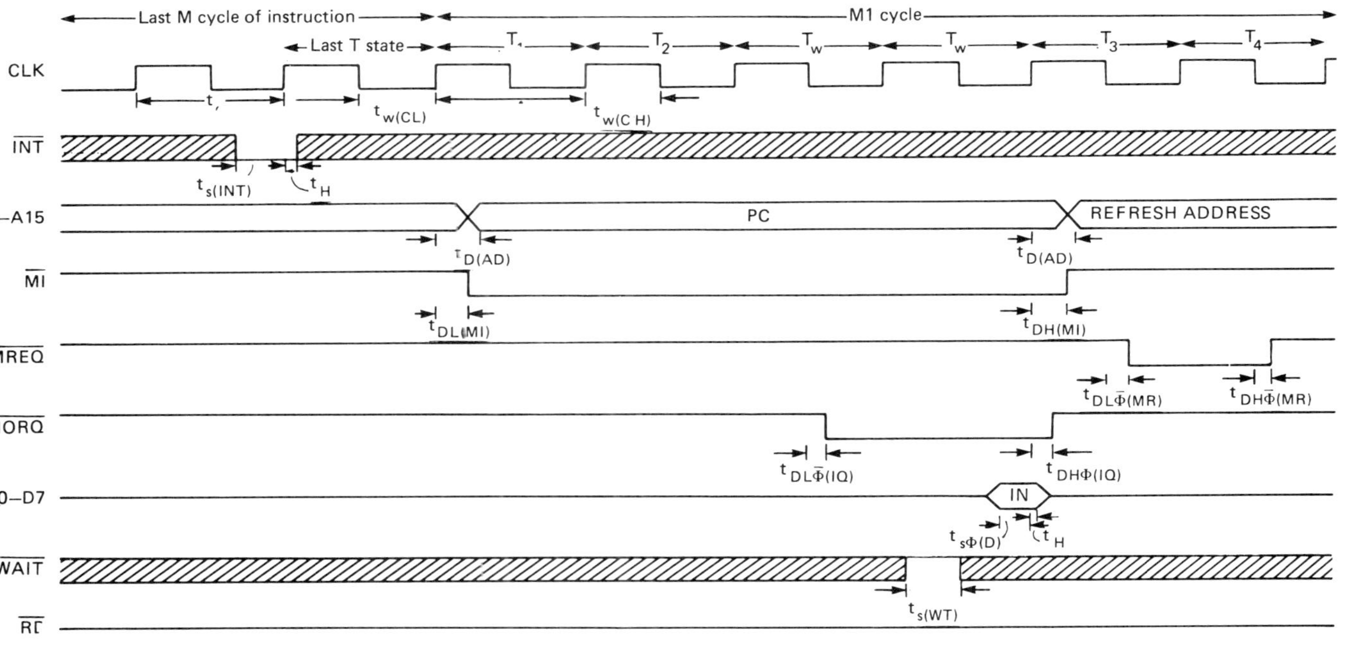

Figure 9.7 Interrupt Request/Acknowledge for a Mode 0/2 interrupt

diagrams are simple to follow. To produce similar types of timing diagrams for other μPs is not too difficult—you just need to be careful that the information you produce is correct and complete.

Note that the wait state occurs between T_2 and T_3. The $\overline{\text{WAIT}}$ input line is polled by the Z80 on the falling edge of T_2. If it is low, then wait states will be inserted until it goes high again. Also note that the setup times and hold times *must* be adhered to.

Figure 9.4 shows the timing for the Instruction fetch operation. This is known as the M1 cycle. $\overline{\text{RFSH}}$ is dependent upon this cycle (the refresh address is made available during T_3 and T_4.). The data is latched by the CPU on the rising edge of T_3. The rising edge of T_3 also turns off the $\overline{\text{RD}}$ and $\overline{\text{MREQ}}$ signals.

Data, in a memory read cycle is latched on the falling edge of T_3.

As can be seen from Figure 9.6, a single wait state is inserted automatically in an I/O cycle. This is in addition to any wait states requested by external devices.

$\overline{\text{INT}}$ is sampled by the CPU on the rising edge of the last T cycle of an instruction. Two wait states are always inserted for an interrupt, whichever mode is being used. $\overline{\text{INT}}$ will be accepted if $\overline{\text{BUSRQ}}$ is high and the Interrupt is not disabled. The three modes for $\overline{\text{INT}}$ are:

Mode 0 The interrupting device places an instruction on the data bus which is read and executed by the CPU. The interrupting device can supply the CPU with any instruction (e.g. a 3 byte call to a particular routine), although single byte restart instructions are most common.

Mode 1 The CPU will automatically jump to location 0038H.

Mode 2 The interrupting device will place a byte on the data bus which will be read by the CPU (the least significant bit must be a 0) and used as the low byte of a 16 bit jump. The high byte comes from the I register and must be stored there by the programmer.

A pulse on $\overline{\text{NMI}}$ sets a latch in the CPU which is tested by the CPU at the end of every instruction (unlike $\overline{\text{INT}}$ which is tested directly).

$\overline{\text{BUSRQ}}$ is sampled by the CPU on the rising edge of the last T state of a machine cycle. Note that $\overline{\text{RFSH}}$ goes tristate when $\overline{\text{BUSRQ}}$ is acknowledged and so if $\overline{\text{BUSRQ}}$ remains active for a long time (>1 ms), the dynamic RAMs may be corrupted.

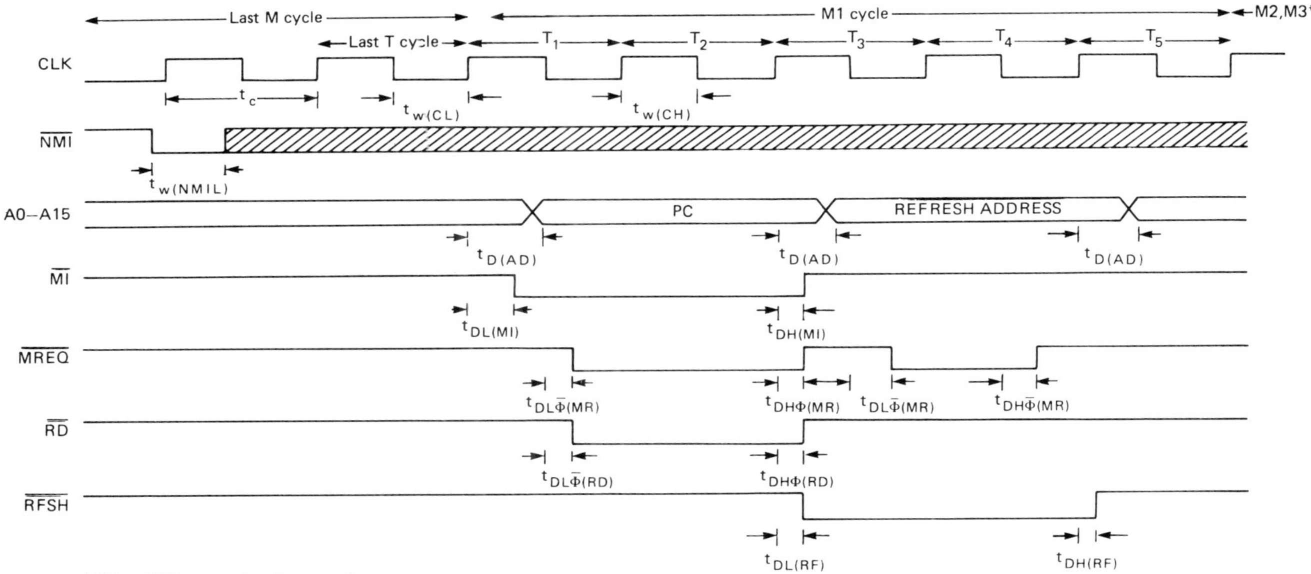

Figure 9.8 Non maskable Interrupt Request/Acknowledge

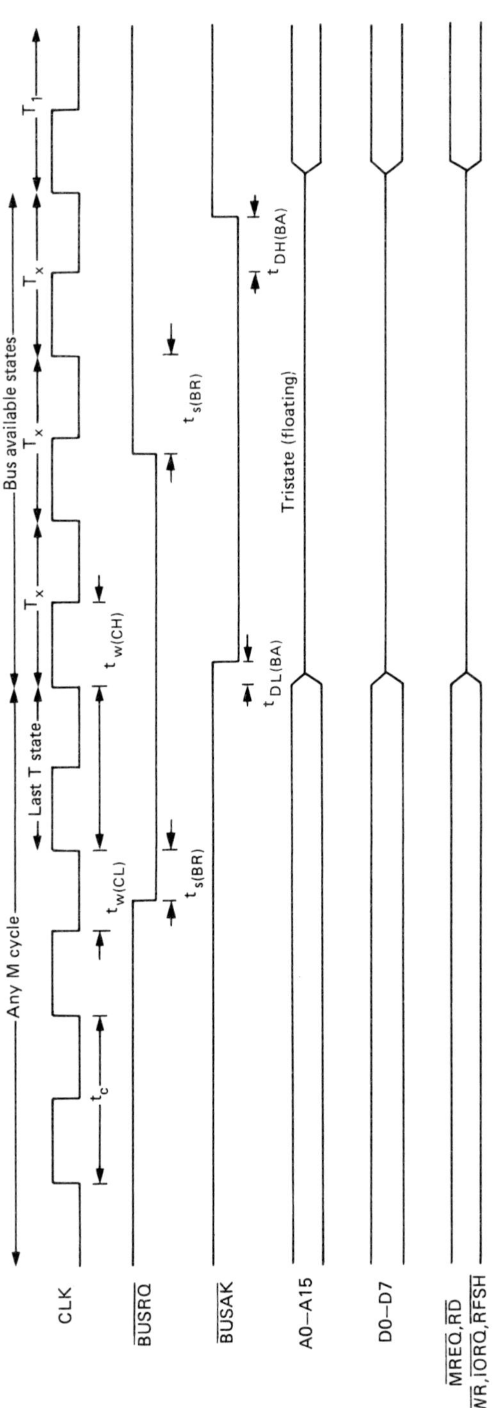

Figure 9.9 Bus Request/Acknowledge

SIGNAL	SYMBOL	PARAMETER	*Z80 CPU*		*Z80A CPU*		*Z80B CPU*	
			Min (ns)	*Max (ns)*	*Min (ns)*	*Max (ns)*	*Min (ns)*	*Max (ns)*
CLK	t_c	Clock period	400	[12]	250	[12]	165	[12]
	$t_{w(\Phi H)}$	Clock pulse width, clock high	180	200us	110	200us	65	200us
	$t_{w(\Phi L)}$	Clock pulse width, clock low	180	2000	110	2000	65	2000
	$t_{r,f}$	Clock rise and fall time		30		30		20
A0–A15	$t_{D(AD)}$	Address output delay		145		110		90
	$t_{f(AD)}$	Delay to float		110		90		80
	t_{acm}	Address stable prior to $\overline{MREQ}$ (memory cycle)	[1]		[13]		[24]	
	t_{aci}	Address stable prior to $\overline{IORQ}$, $\overline{RD}$ or $\overline{WR}$ (I/O cycle)	[2]		[14]		[25]	
	t_{ca}	Address stable from $\overline{RD}$, $\overline{WR}$, $\overline{IORQ}$ or $\overline{MREQ}$	[3]		[15]		[26]	
	t_{caf}	Address stable from $\overline{RD}$ or $\overline{WR}$ during float	[4]		[16]		[27]	
D0–D7	$t_{D(D)}$	Data output delay		230		150		130
	$t_{F(D)}$	Delay to float during write cycle		90		90		80
	$t_{S\Phi(D)}$	Data setup time to rising edge of clock during M1	50		35		30	
	$t_{S\bar{\Phi}(D)}$	Data setup time to rising edge of clock during M2–M5	60		50		40	
	t_{dcm}	Data stable prior ro $\overline{WR}$ (Memory cycle)	[5]		[17]		[28]	
	t_{dci}	Data stable prior to $\overline{WR}$ (I/O cycle)	[6]		[18]		[29]	
	t_{cdf}	Data stable from $\overline{WR}$	[7]		[19]		[30]	
	t_H	Input hold time	0		0		0	
$\overline{MREQ}$	$t_{DL\bar{\Phi}(MR)}$	$\overline{MREQ}$ delay from falling edge of clock, $\overline{MREQ}$ low	20	100	20	85	20	70
	$t_{DH\Phi(MR)}$	$\overline{MREQ}$ delay from rising edge of clock, $\overline{MREQ}$ high		100		85		70
	$t_{DH\bar{\Phi}(MR)}$	$\overline{MREQ}$ delay from falling edge of clock, $\overline{MREQ}$ high		100		85		70
	$t_{w(\overline{MRL})}$	Pulse width, $\overline{MREQ}$ low	[8]		[20]		[20]	
	$t_{w(\overline{MRH})}$	Pulse width, $\overline{MREQ}$ high	[9]		[21]		[21]	

$\overline{IORQ}$	$t_{DL\Phi(IR)}$	$\overline{IORQ}$ delay from rising edge of clock, $\overline{IORQ}$ low		90		75		65
	$t_{DL\bar{\Phi}(IR)}$	$\overline{IORQ}$ delay from falling edge of clock, $\overline{IORQ}$ low		110		85		70
	$t_{DH\Phi(IR)}$	$\overline{IORQ}$ delay from rising edge of clock, $\overline{IORQ}$ high		100		85		70
	$t_{DH\bar{\Phi}(IR)}$	$\overline{IORQ}$ delay from falling edge of clock, $\overline{IORQ}$ high		110		85		70
$\overline{RD}$	$t_{DL\Phi(RD)}$	$\overline{RD}$ delay from rising edge of clock, $\overline{RD}$ low		100		85		70
	$t_{DL\bar{\Phi}(RD)}$	$\overline{RD}$ delay from falling edge of clock, $\overline{RD}$ low		130		95		80
	$t_{DH\Phi(RD)}$	$\overline{RD}$ delay from rising edge of clock, $\overline{RD}$ high	15	100	15	85	15	70
	$t_{DH\bar{\Phi}(RD)}$	$\overline{RD}$ delay from falling edge of clock, $\overline{RD}$ high		110		85		70
$\overline{WR}$	$t_{DL\Phi(WR)}$	$\overline{WR}$ delay from rising edge of clock, $\overline{WR}$ low		80		65		60
	$t_{DL\bar{\Phi}(WR)}$	$\overline{WR}$ delay from falling edge of clock, $\overline{WR}$ low		90		80		70
	$t_{DH\Phi(WR)}$	$\overline{WR}$ delay from falling edge of clock, $\overline{WR}$ high		100		80		70
	$t_{DH\bar{\Phi}(WR)}$	Pulse width, $\overline{WR}$ low	[10]		[22]		[22]	
$\overline{M1}$	$t_{DL(M1)}$	$\overline{M1}$ delay from rising edge of clock, $\overline{M1}$ low		130		100		80
	$t_{DH\ (M1)}$	$\overline{M1}$ delay from rising edge of clock, $\overline{M1}$ high		130		100		80
$\overline{RFSH}$	$t_{DL(RF)}$	$\overline{RFSH}$ delay from rising edge of clock, $\overline{RFSH}$ low		180		130		110
	$t_{DH(RF)}$	$\overline{RFSH}$ delay from rising edge of clock, $\overline{RFSH}$ high		150		120		100
$\overline{WAIT}$	$t_{S(WT)}$	$\overline{WAIT}$ setup time to falling edge of clock	70		70		60	
$\overline{HALT}$	$t_{D(HT)}$	$\overline{HALT}$ delay time from falling edge of clock		300		300		260
$\overline{INT}$	$t_{S(IT)}$	$\overline{INT}$ setup time to rising edge of clock	80		80		70	
$\overline{NMI}$	$t_{W(\overline{NML})}$	Pulse width, $\overline{NMI}$ low	80		80		70	
$\overline{BURSQ}$	$t_{S(BQ)}$	$\overline{BURSQ}$ setup time to rising edge of clock	80		50		50	
$\overline{BUSAK}$	$t_{DL(BA)}$	$\overline{BUSAK}$ delay from rising edge of clock, $\overline{BUSAK}$ low		120		100		90
	$t_{DH(BA)}$	$\overline{BUSAK}$ delay from falling edge of clock, $\overline{BUSAK}$ high		110		100		90
$\overline{RESET}$	$t_{S(RS)}$	$\overline{RESET}$ setup time to rising edge of clock	90		60		60	
	$t_{F(C)}$	Delay to/from float ($\overline{MREQ}$, $\overline{IORQ}$, $\overline{RD}$ and $\overline{WR}$)		100		80		70
	t_{mr}	M1 stable prior to $\overline{IORQ}$ (Interrupt Acknowledge)	[11]		[23]		[31]	

[1] $t_{acm}=t_{w(\Phi H)}+t_f-75$
[2] $t_{aci}=t_c-80$
[3] $t_{ca}=t_{w(\Phi L)}+t_r-40$
[4] $t_{caf}=t_{w(\Phi L)}+t_r-60$
[5] $t_{dcm}=t_c-210$
[6] $t_{dci}=t_{w(\Phi L)}+t_r-210$
[7] $t_{cdf}=t_{w(\Phi L)}+t_r-80$
[8] $t_{w(\overline{MRL})}=t_c-40$
[9] $t_{w(\overline{MRM})}=t_{w(\Phi H)}+t_f-30$
[10] $t_{w(\overline{WR})}=t_c-40$
[11] $t_{mr}=2t_c+t_{w(\Phi H)}+t_f-80$
[12] $t_c=t_{w(\Phi H)}+t_{w(\Phi C)}+t_r+t_f$
[13] $t_{acm}=t_{w(\Phi H)}+t_f-65$
[14] $t_{aci}=t_c-70$
[15] $t_{ca}=t_{w(\Phi L)}+t_r-50$
[16] $t_{caf}=t_{w(\Phi L)}+t_r-45$
[17] $t_{dcm}=t_c-170$
[18] $t_{dci}=t_{w(\Phi L)}+t_r-170$
[19] $t_{cdf}=t_{w(\Phi L)}+t_r-70$
[20] $t_{w(\overline{MRL})}=t_c-30$
[21] $t_{w(\overline{MRH})}=t_{w(\Phi H)}+t_f-20$
[22] $t_{w(\overline{WR})}=t_c-30$
[23] $t_{mr}=2t_c+t_{w(\Phi H)}+t_f-65$
[24] $t_{acm}=t_{w(\Phi H)}+t_f-50$
[25] $t_{aci}=t_c-55$
[26] $t_{ca}=t_{w(\Phi L)}+t_r-50$
[27] $t_{caf}=t_{w(\Phi L)}+t_r-45$
[28] $t_{dcm}=t_c-140$
[29] $t_{dci}=t_{w(\Phi L)}+t_r-140$
[30] $t_{cdf}=t_{w(\Phi L)}+t_r-55$
[31] $t_{mr}=2t_c+t_{w(\Phi H)}+t_r-50$

9.6.2 Z80 Instruction Set

The Z80 can execute 158 different instruction types. To go over the full range would take too long—the reader is advised to buy a book on Assembly language programming for the Z80.

9.7 16 BIT MICROPROCESSORS

16 bit microprocessors are much more powerful than 8 bit microprocessors. In this section, I shall merely compare the three most common 16 bit μPs. For further details, there are many books available on the subject. Table 9.5 gives the three most common 16 bit μPs and Table 9.6 compares them.

Name	*Manufacturer*
68000	Motorola
8086	Intel
Z8000	Zilog

Table 9.5 Most common 16 bit μPs

Feature	*68000*	*8086*	*Z8000*
Addressing modes	14	24	8
Size of registers	32 bit	16 bit	16 bit
No. of registers	17	14	16
Max. clock frequency	12 MHz	10 MHz	4 MHz
Number of Interrupts	7	2	2
Address range	16 Mbytes	1 Mbyte	8 Mbytes

Table 9.6 Comparison of most common 16 bit μPs

The comparison in Table 9.6 is very brief, but should be enough to give the reader an idea of how 16 bit μPs work.

9.8 HIGH LEVEL LANGUAGES (HLL)

An HLL is more understandable than Assembly language and hence is easier to write. Also HLL programs may be run on virtually any microprocessor, provided that a translator for the particular microprocessor exists. A translator which converts a program into machine code is called a compiler. A translator which converts the code line by line and executes each line after it has been translated is called an Interpreter. Compiled programs run faster than Interpreted programs. Interpreters are easier to write than Compilers and hence are cheaper. Examples of HLLs are FORTRAN, BASIC, PASCAL, C, APL, etc.

An example of a program to add two numbers together using BASIC is shown in Figure 9.10.

```
10 INPUT A
20 INPUT B
30 C=A+B
40 PRINT C
```

Figure 9.10 Program to add two numbers together using BASIC

BASIC uses line numbers to tell the interpreter/compiler which line to translate next.

There are many books on programming in HLLs—they are useful reading.

9.9 CONCLUSION

After reading this chapter you should have a very good feel for how microprocessors work. In particular, you should now be able to design with the Z80 CPU. The next two chapters will introduce microprocessor support devices and memories, after which you will be able to design your own microcomputer system.

10
Memories

A memory is a device which can store and retrieve information. There are seven main types of memory available and they are listed below:

RAM	(Random Access) Read/Write Memory
ROM	(Random Access) Read Only Memory
Cassette Tape	(Sequential Access) Read/Write Storage Memory
Floppy Disk	(Random Access) Read/Write Storage Memory
Hard Disk	(Random Access) Read/Write Storage Memory
Magnetic Tape	(Sequential Access) Read/Write Storage Memory
Bubble	(Random Access) Read/Write Storage Memory

RAM is the fastest type of memory device and is widely used in computers as program memory. RAM devices lose their information when they are switched off—hence the need for storage memories.

ROM is used in computers to store permanent programs, e.g. the operating system program, word processors, etc.

Cassette tapes are the cheapest storage devices available and run at 300 baud (bits per second), which corresponds to approximately 30 characters per second, or 1200 baud (120 characters per second). The disadvantages of cassette tape are twofold:

1. The access to stored programs is sequential i.e. if the program desired is at the end of the tape, you must go through all of the tape to get to it.
2. The transfer rate from RAM to cassette is slow.

Floppy disks are widely used in small computer systems and have a much faster transfer rate than cassette tapes. They are also more reliable (less prone to transfer errors). However their great advantage over cassettes is that the access to the stored programs is random, i.e. any part of the floppy disk may be accessed without needing to go through all of the preceding data.

Hard disks are used in larger computer systems and have a much higher storage capacity and a faster transfer rate than floppy disks. They are also much more expensive.

Magnetic tape and bubble memories are not used much in small computer systems and shall not be discussed in this book.

Table 10.1 compares the various types of memory.

Memory	*Typical storage*	*Cost*	*Transfer rate*
RAM	Up to 256 Kbits per IC (1985)	Up to £50 per IC (Average £3)	2 million to 10 million chars/sec.
ROM	Up to 512 Kbits per IC (1985)	Up to £50 per IC (Average £3)	As for RAM
Cassette	650 Kbytes per 90 min. tape	Approx. £25 +£1 per tape	30–120 chars/sec.
Floppy Disk	100–1000 Kbytes per diskette	Approx. £200+ £3 per diskette	15625–62500 chars/sec.
Hard Disk	5–140 Mbytes (1985)	Approx. £800+	625,000 chars/sec.

Table 10.1 Comparison between memories

Note that, in relation to memories, K=1024 and M=1024×1024. Also note that as RAM/ROM sizes increase, the access times tend to increase. Hence a very small ROM may have a much faster access time than a large ROM.

10.1 RAM

There are three types of RAM:

1. Static MOS RAM
2. Dynamic RAM
3. Bipolar RAM

10.1.1 Static MOS RAM (SRAM)

This is a MOS device which is accessed by addressing the exact location that is to be read or written to. There are many types of static RAM:

1K × 1
1K × 4
2K × 8
etc.

A 1K × 1 RAM has 1024 addresses, each of which contains 1 data bit.

A 2K × 8 RAM has 2048 addresses, each of which contains 8 data bits, and which are accessed in parallel.

Figure 10.1 shows a representation for a 1K × 1 RAM and a 2K × 8 RAM.

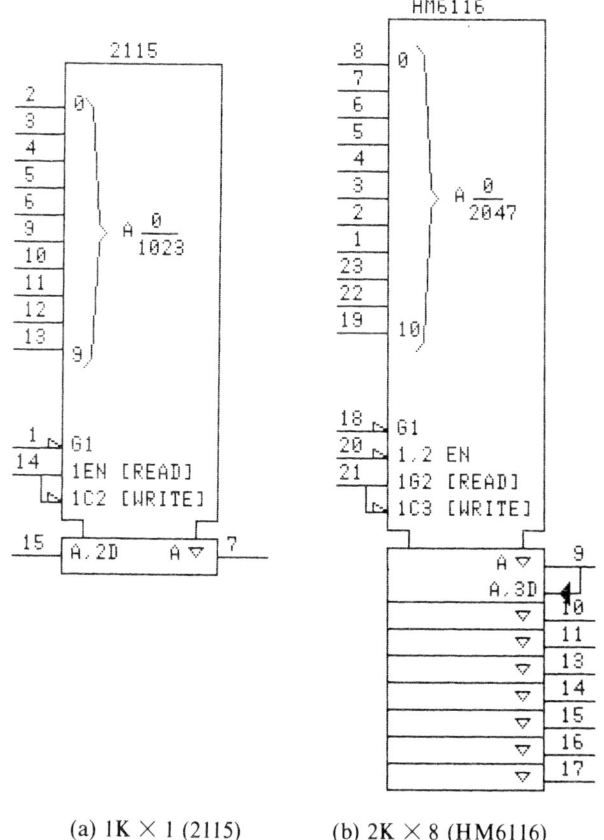

(a) 1K × 1 (2115) (b) 2K × 8 (HM6116)

Figure 10.1 Representation of 1K × 1 RAM and 2K × 8 RAM

As seen in Figure 10.1, some data lines are bidirectional and some are unidirectional.

For the 2115, the pin functions are as follows:

A0–A9	Unidirectional address bus (Input)
DIN	Data Input (unidirectional)
DOUT	Data Output (unidirectional)
$\overline{\text{WE}}$	Write Enable (Input)
$\overline{\text{CS}}$	Chip Select

The operation of the device is as follows:

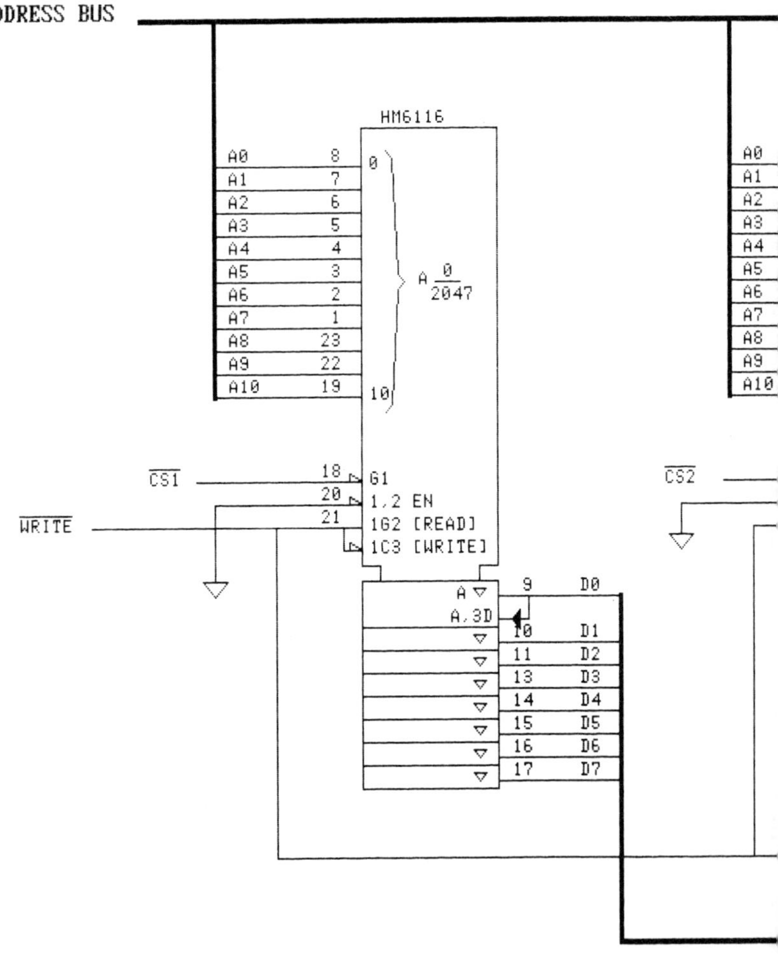

Figure 10.2 Bank of three HM6116 RAMs

If $\overline{CS}$ is low, then Control 1 is active and hence the $\overline{WE}$ input is enabled.

If $\overline{WE}$ is enabled and is low, then Control 2 is active and the data on the DIN line will be stored at the address referenced by the address bus. During this, the DOUT line is tristated (as seen by the ▽). If $\overline{WE}$ is high, then the EN is active. Hence ▽ becomes inactive and DOUT will display the data stored at the address referenced by the address bus.

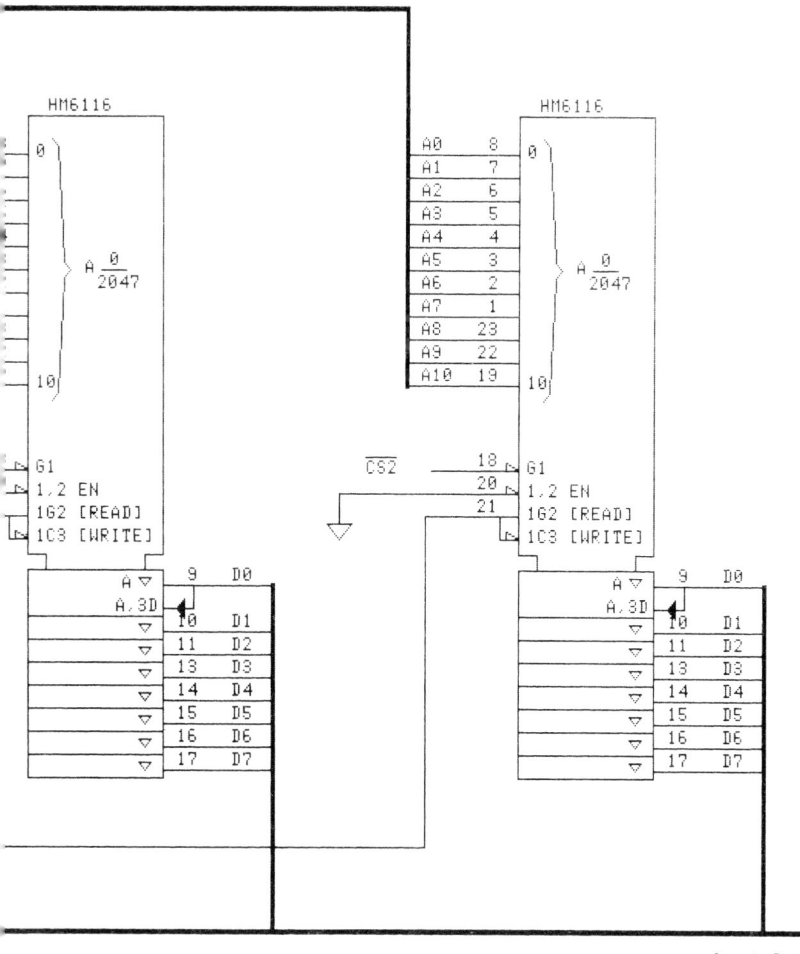

For the exact timing, see the Intel data book or any data book that has the 2115 in it.

The pin functions for the HM6116 are as follows:

A0–A10	Unidirectional address bus (Input)
D0–D7	Bidirectional data bus (Input/Output)
$\overline{\text{WE}}$	Write Enable
$\overline{\text{CE}}$	Chip Enable
$\overline{\text{OE}}$	Output Enable

The operation of the HM6116 is shown in Table 10.2

$\overline{\text{CE}}$	$\overline{\text{OE}}$	$\overline{\text{WE}}$	D0–D7
H	X	X	Z
L	X	L	DIN
L	L	H	DOUT
L	H	H	Z

Table 10.2 Operation of HM6116

Explanation of new logic symbol

This is very similar to the 2115. The major difference is the way in which the bidirectional bus is shown.

Z means high impedence (tristate)—effectively the IC is disconnected from the circuit. This is useful if you have banks of RAMs, all at different addresses, which use the same data bus. An example of this is shown in Figure 10.2.

Depending on which select line is low, one RAM device will be selected.

The bus structure is a common one. There are various ways to show connections to a bus. Two common ways are shown in Figure 10.3.

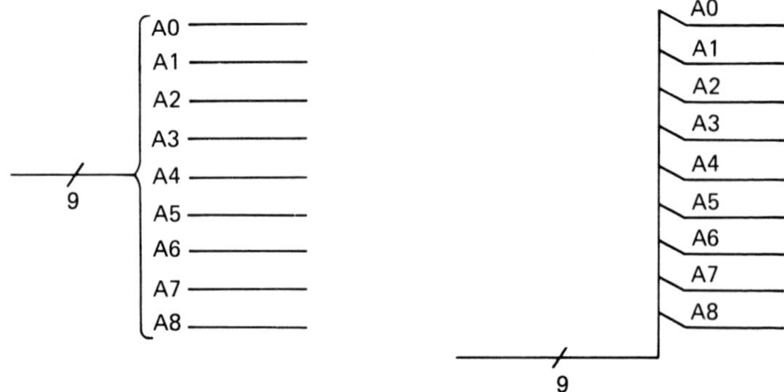

Figure 10.3 Two ways of showing connections to a bus

Note: EVERY TIME A BUS BRANCHES, ALWAYS PUT THE NUMBER OF SIGNALS ON EACH BRANCH, as shown in Figure 10.2.

10.1.2 Dynamic RAM (DRAM)

This is a MOS device.

Dynamic RAMs are easier to make than Static RAMs. They are also smaller. The reason for this is that they use more simple logic. Their disadvantage is that each address cell needs to be refreshed at least once every 2 ms.

A dynamic RAM is arranged in a matrix fashion with rows and columns. To economize on pins, the address bits are multiplexed and a Row Address Strobe (RAS) and Column Address Strobe (CAS) are provided to latch the address bits. Hence to access an address cell, first the row address is put onto the address inputs and RAS made low and then the column address is put onto the address inputs and CAS made low.

To refresh the whole RAM, every row address must be accessed at least once every 2 ms.

You can design circuitry around the DRAM to do the RAS and CAS timing and also to do the refreshing. This is tedious and uses a lot of ICs. However there are ICs which will do all of this. These ICs are called Dynamic RAM controllers. A 64K × 1 DRAM and a DRAM controller are shown in Figure 10.4.

Note that the dependence notation symbol for the 4164 is quite complicated. Accordingly, it is easier to draw the 4164 as in Figure 10.4 (b). In general, as the complexity of the IC gets greater, the more complicated to draw (and less useful) the dependency symbol becomes. I shall not give dependency symbols for the 8203 or for more complicated devices—the reader may work out symbols as an exercise.

Once the DRAMs are connected to the DRAM controller, they almost appear like SRAMs to the system. However, separate refresh circuitry is needed. A typical 64K × 8 DRAM block is shown in Figure 10.5.

Note the series damping resistors (mentioned in Chapter 5—analog components). These are used to prevent the combined capacitance of the DRAMs from slowing the signals down too much. ALWAYS USE SERIES DAMPING RESISTORS IN THIS FASHION WHEN DEALING WITH MOS MEMORY ARRAYS.

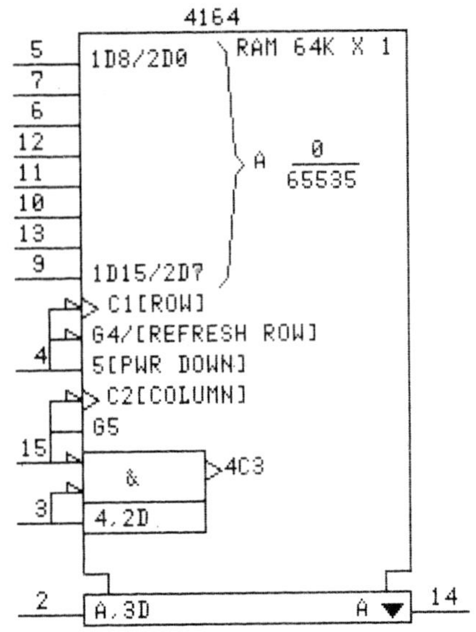

(a) 4164 symbol in dependency notation

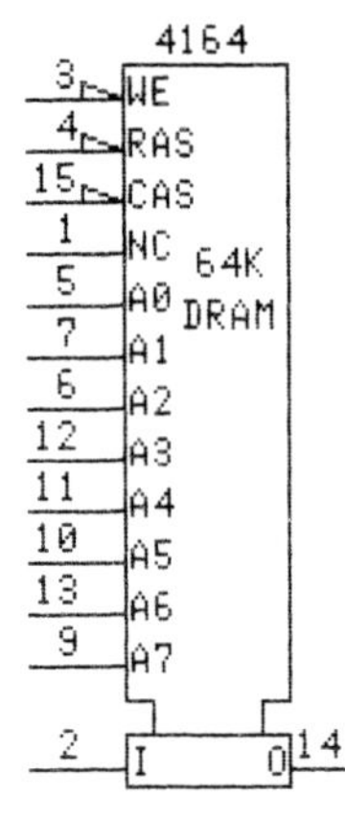

(b) 4164 64K × 1 DRAM

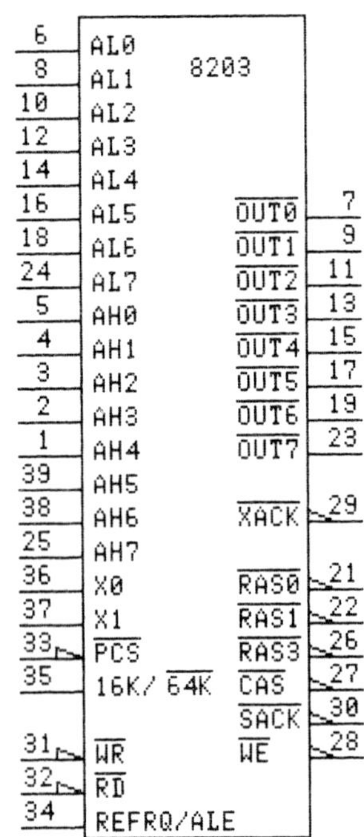

(c) 8203 64K DRAM controller

Figure 10.4 4164 DRAM and 8203 DRAM controller

Also note how the 8 DRAMs are shown. Since they have common control signals, it is easier to join them together with a common control block than to keep them separate.

10.1.3 Bipolar RAM

These are high speed TTL (not MOS) devices. Their storage capacity is much lower than static or dynamic RAM. They are static in operation and are used in high speed applications. An example of a Bipolar RAM is the 74S189, whose circuit symbol is shown in Figure 10.6. The 74S189 is a 64 bit RAM, organised as 16×4 i.e. 16 locations each 4 bits wide. Four address inputs are required for 16 locations ($16=2^4$). The access time for a 74S189 is 25 ns max i.e. data may be read or written 25 ns after the address and enable lines are stable.

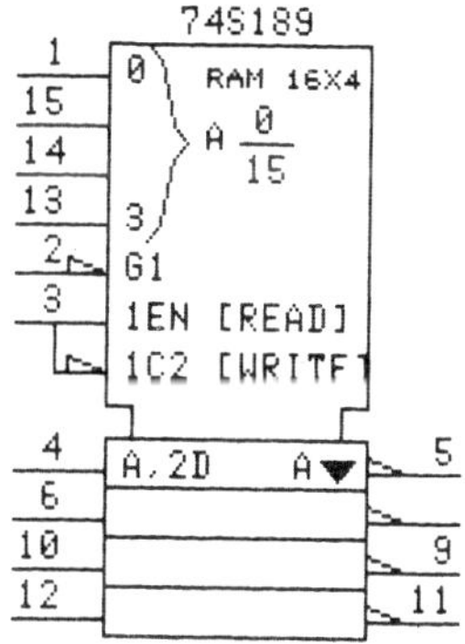

Figure 10.6 Circuit symbol for 74S189

10.2 ROM

There are six types of ROM:

1. ROM
2. PROM
3. Bipolar PROM
4. EPROM
5. EEPROM (EAROM)
6. Programmable Logic Array (PLA).

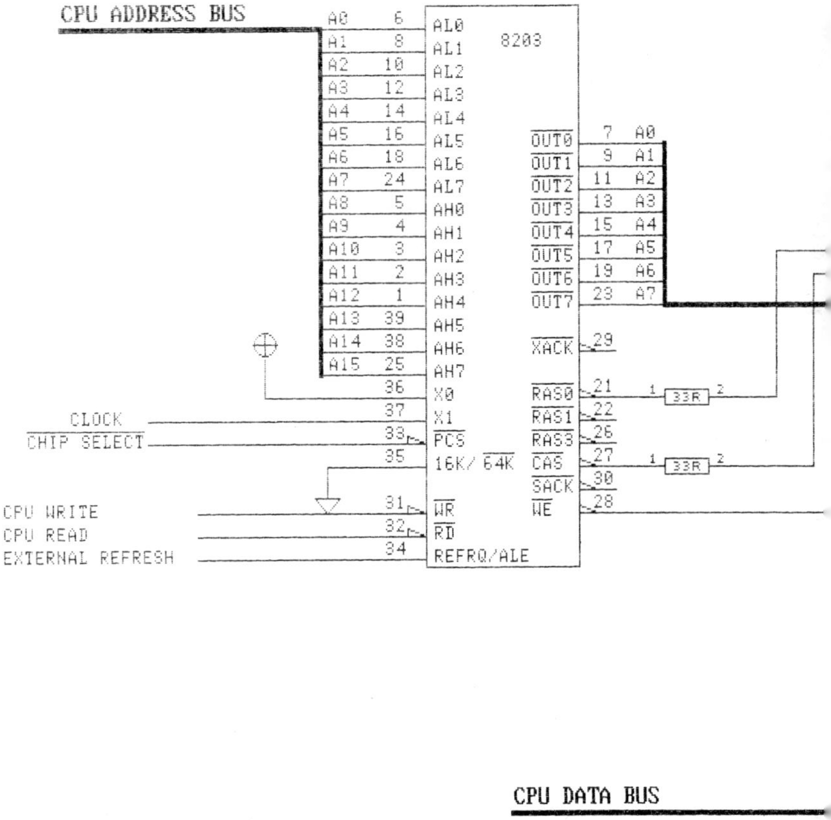

Figure 10.5 64K × 8 DRAM block

10.2.1 ROM (Read Only Memory)

These devices are programmed when they are made. There is no way to change their contents.

10.2.2 PROM (Programmable Read Only Memory)

These devices can be programmed using a PROM programmer. Once they have been programmed, there is no way to change their contents.

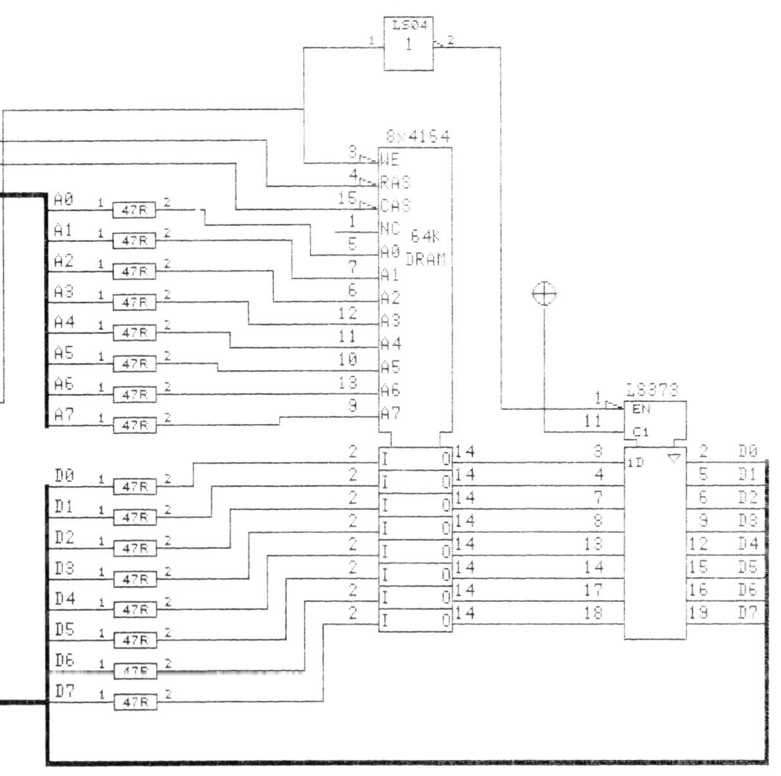

10.2.3 Bipolar PROMs

These are TTL PROMs which all have very fast access time (typically 50 ns to 70 ns as opposed to 200 ns upwards for normal PROMs). An example of a bipolar PROM is the 74288 whose circuit symbol is shown in Figure 10.7. The 74S288 is a 256 bit PROM arranged as 32×8, i.e. 32 locations each 8 bits wide. Five address bits are required for 32 locations ($32=2^5$). The access time for a 74S288 is 70 ns.

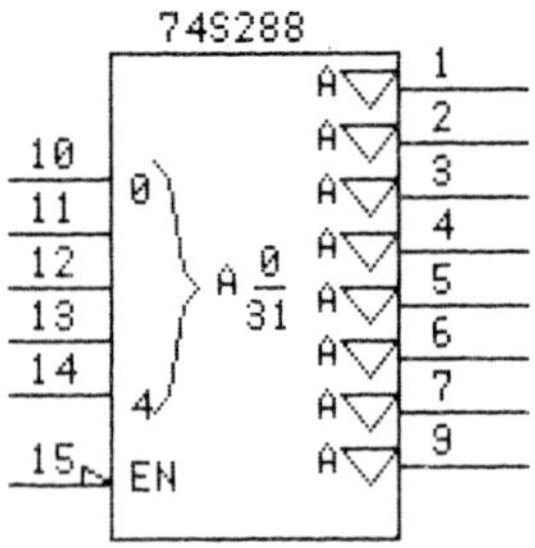

Figure 10.7 Circuit symbol for 74S288

10.2.4 EPROM (Erasable Programmable Read Only Memory)

These devices can be programmed using a PROM programmer. They may be erased by ultraviolet light. Do not leave them in direct sunlight (which contains UV light). These devices may be reprogrammed up to 1000 times. An example of an EPROM is the 2764, whose circuit symbol is shown in Figure 10.8. The 2764 is a 64 Kbit EPROM arranged as 8K × 8 i.e. 8192 locations, each 8 bits wide. Thirteen address inputs are required for 8K locations ($8192=2^{13}$). The access time for a 2764 can be 250 ns or 450 ns, depending on the version of 2764.

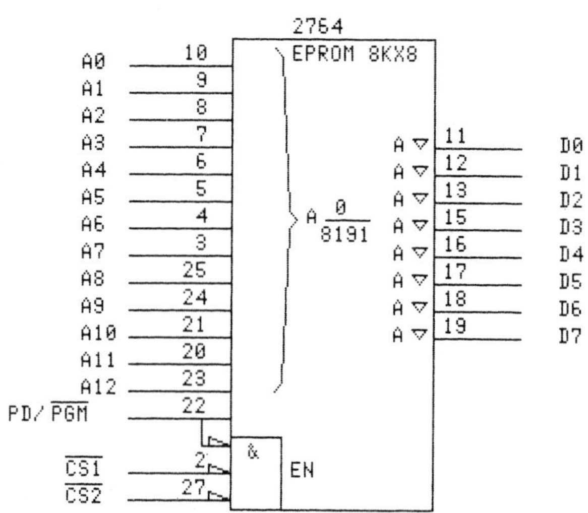

Figure 10.8 Circuit symbol for 2764

10.2.5 EEPROM (Electrically Erasable PROM) or EAROM (Electrically Alterable ROM)

After these devices have been programmed, they can be changed by merely reprogramming them. It is not necessary to use UV light as for EPROMs.

10.2.6 PLAs

A PLA is a device which allows the inputs to influence the outputs via a limited logic array. PLAs are normally split up into five stages:

1. Input lines (usually include feedback from the output lines)
2. AND matrix
3. OR matrix
4. Storage element (not always present)
5. Output lines.

Any input line (or output line if feedback is permitted) may be ANDed with any other input line in the AND matrix. This is done by "blowing" appropriate fuses in the PLA. The AND matrix will allow a certain number of terms (different combinations of input lines), typically 16 to 64. Each of these terms can contain any number of input lines (including their inverses). These AND terms are then passed on, in a similar fashion, to the OR matrix. The OR matrix may either be fixed, or programmable. If it is fixed, then certain AND lines are automatically ORed together to produce the outputs. If the OR matrix is programmable, then the OR terms can contain any number of the AND terms.

Some PLAs have storage elements (D type flip flops) immediately after the OR terms. These "registered" PLAs can be very useful.

Three examples of PLAs are shown in Figures 10.9 to 10.11. Figure 10.9 shows a fixed OR array with six array inputs and one output. As can be seen, there are only two real inputs to the PLA. There are four AND terms involved, each of which can contain any combination of Input 1, Input 2, Output or their inverses. These four AND terms are then ORed together and fed back into the PLA as well as going to the output. Initially every vertical line is connected to each of the AND term lines via a fuse. To disconnect one vertical line from an AND term line, all that is necessary is to blow the appropriate fuse.

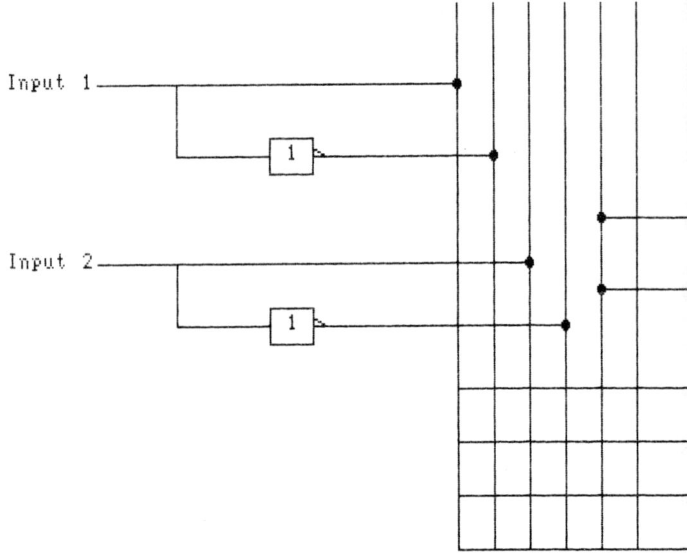

Figure 10.9 Six input, one output fixed OR PLA

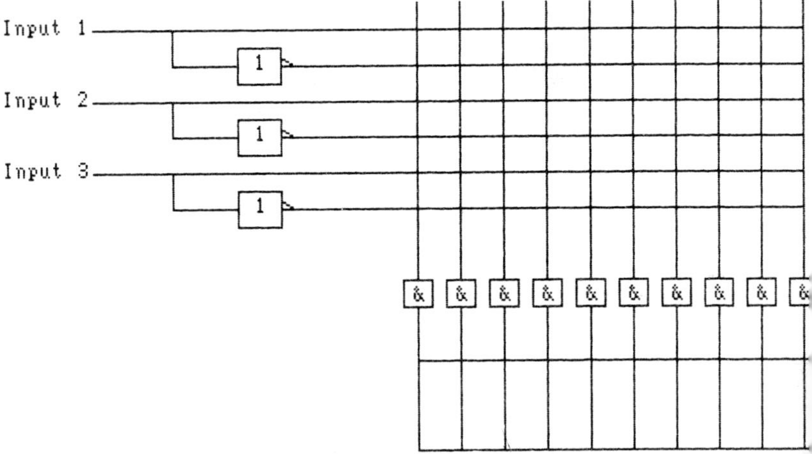

Figure 10.10 3 × 10 × 2 PLA

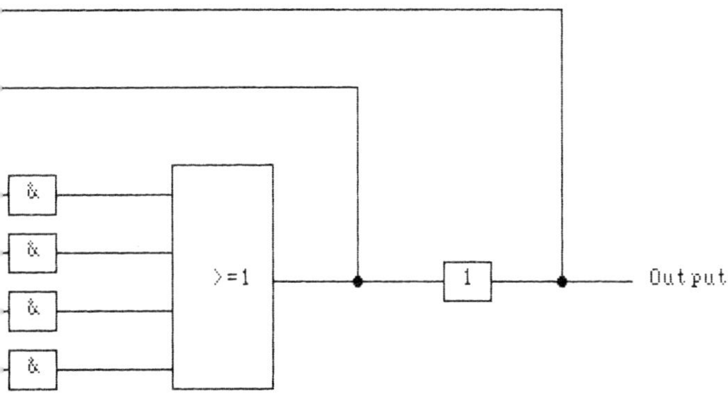
&
&
&
&
>=1
1
Output

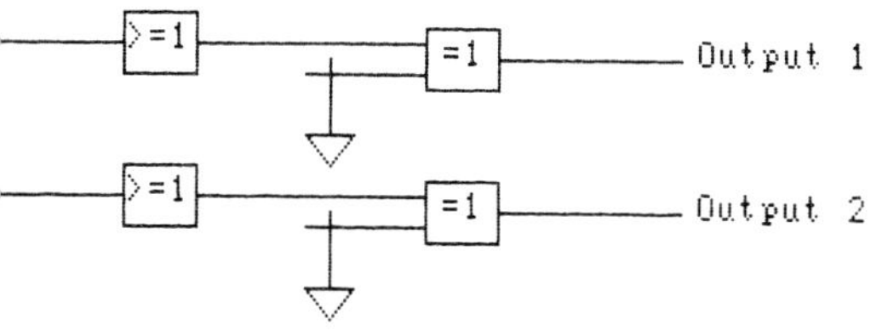
>=1
=1
Output 1
>=1
=1
Output 2

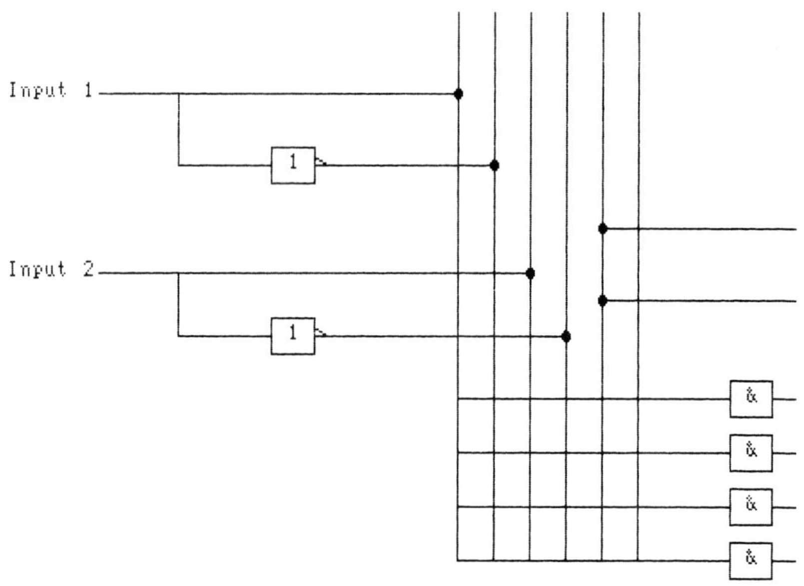

Figure 10.11 Registered six input, one output fixed OR PLA

Figure 10.10 shows a 3 × 10 × 2 PLA. The 3 refers to the number of inputs, the 10 refers to the number of AND terms and the 2 refers to the number of OR terms (and hence outputs). Any of the crossing lines may be connected together by not blowing the appropriate fuses involved.

Note that both of the outputs can have fuses blown to make them active high or active low.

Figure 10.11 shows a registered six input, one output fixed OR PLA. This is identical to Figure 10.9, except that the output of the OR stage goes into a D type flip flop which is clocked externally.

PLAs are useful for replacing SSI TTL in applications where the chip count (number of ICs on a Printed Circuit Board) needs to be kept to a minimum. They are also useful for discouraging people from copying your design!

PLAs are also known as PALs or FPLAs (Field Programmable Logic Arrays).

Texas Instruments' Bipolar Microcomputer Components Data Book has details on some PLAs, as well as bipolar RAMs and ROMs.

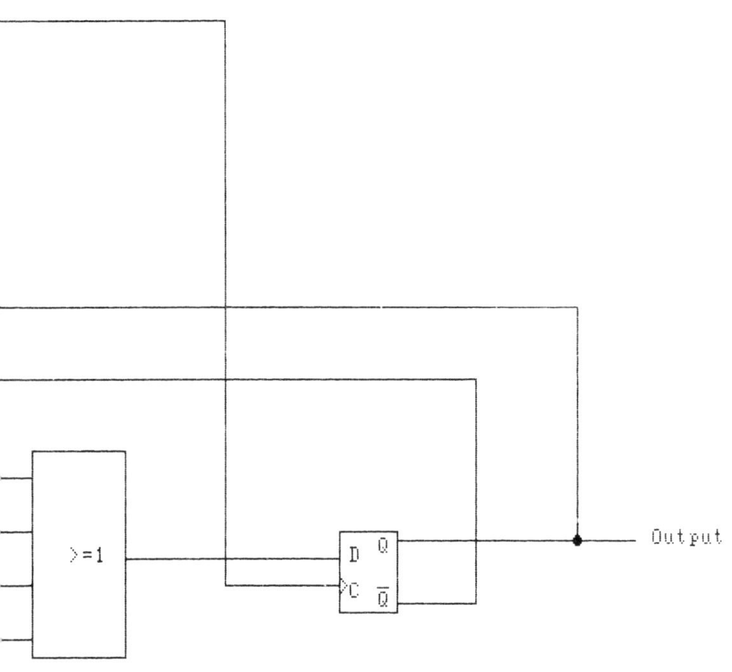

Plate 9 5¼″ diskette and floppy disk drive

10.3 FLOPPY DISKS

A 5¼″ floppy disk drive is shown in Plate 9 along with a diskette. The diskette fits into the drive with the tab on the left hand side, facing upwards. This tab is the write protect tab. When covered, the diskette cannot be written to.

There are two main types of floppy disk—5¼″ and 8″. A third type (3″—3½″) is being developed at the moment.

There are many floppy disk interface ICs which are easy to use. One of these is Intel's 8272 (NEC's μPD765A is an equivalent). The 8272 is shown in Figure 10.12.

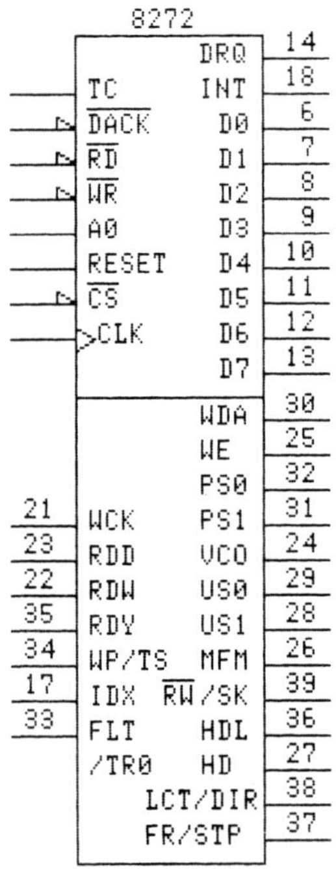

Figure 10.12 8272 Floppy Disk Controller (FDC)

The function of each pin is described below:

A0	(Input) Selects data register (A0=1) or status register (A0=0).
DB0–DB7	(I/O) Bidirectional data bus.

IDX	(Input, activate high) IDX is high at the beginning of a disk track.
WCK	(Input) WCK is a pulse train @ 500 kHz for FM (single density diskettes) and @ 1 MHz for MFM (double density diskettes). The pulse width is 250 ns.
RDD	(Input) Data In from the data separator.
FLT/TR0	(Input, active high). This is high for a fault condition in read/write mode and is high when track 0 is found in seek mode.
WP/TS	(Input, active high). This is high if the diskette is write protected in read/write mode and is high when side 2 is being accessed in seek mode.
RDY	(Input, active high). This is high when the FDD is ready to send or receive data.
WE	(Output, active high). When high this enables write data into FDD.
HDL	(Output, active high). When high the FDD will lower the read/write head onto the diskette.
US1,US0	(Output). These two lines select one of four FDDs.
WDA	(Output). This sends serial data and clock bits to the FDD.
PS1,PS0	(Output). These two lines give the precompensation status during MFM mode.
HD	(Output). Selects head 0 when 0 and head 1 when 1 (there are two heads on double sided FDDs).
FR/STP	(Output, active high). When high in read/write mode, this resets the fault flip flop in the FDD. When high in seek mode, this enables the step pulses to move the head to another cylinder.
LCT/DIR	(Output, active high). When high in read/write mode, this lowers the write current on the inner tracks. When high in seek mode, then the direction in which the head will step is inwards (when low, the direction is outwards).

$\overline{\text{RW}}$/SEEK (Output). When high, seek mode is selected and when low, read/write mode is selected.

RDW (Input). Data In clock from data separator.

VCO (Output). Inhibits VCO (Voltage Controlled Oscillator) in PLL when 0 and enables it when 1.

MFM (Output). MFM mode when 1, FM mode when 0.

$\overline{\text{RD}}$ (Input, active low). $\overline{\text{RD}}$ signal from CPU.

$\overline{\text{WR}}$ (Input, active low). $\overline{\text{WR}}$ signal from CPU.

$\overline{\text{CS}}$ (Input, active low). Chip Select signal.

CLK (Input). 8 MHz square wave clock.

RST (Input, active high). Resets all lines to FDD to 0.

INT (Output, active high). Interrupt Request to CPU.

$\overline{\text{DACK}}$ (Input, active low). DMA cycle is active when $\overline{\text{DACK}}$ is low.

TC (Input, active high). TC is high at the end of a DMA transfer.

DRQ (Output, active high). DRQ is high when FDC requests DMA transfer.

A circuit demonstrating the use of an 8272 is shown in Figure 10.13.

The 9216 is a device called a data separator. Its function is to separate the mixed clock and data which the floppy disk drive supplies. The floppy disk drive signals are explained below. These signals are typical to most 5¼″ drives:

Drive n Select (n=0 to 3)
These signals enable one of up to 4 drives.

Side This signal choses between side 0 and side 1 of a double sided drive.

Motor On This signal will turn the drive motor on and off.

Direction As defined for the 8272.

Step As defined for the 8272.

Write Data As for WDA on 8272.

Write Enable As for WE on 8272.

Index	As for IDX on 8272.
Track 0	As for FLT/TR0 on 8272.
Ready	As for RDY on 8272.
Read Data	This is the combined data in/clock from the drive. This line is separated by the 9216 into the data and the data clock.
Write Protect	When high, the diskette in the drive has a write protect tab and may not be written to.

The circuit in Figure 10.13 should be fairly self explanatory. For more details on floppy disk drives, the reader is advised to read the Intel data book (8271, 8272 supplementary details) or a specialist book on the subject.

Hard disks are not discussed in detail here, but their use and applications are similar to floppy disks.

10.4 CONCLUSION

Memory devices are essential to any computer system. The reader should now feel confident enough to design the basis of a microcomputer system (μP, ROM, MSI and SSI). The next thing to learn is how to interface the microcomputer to the outside world.

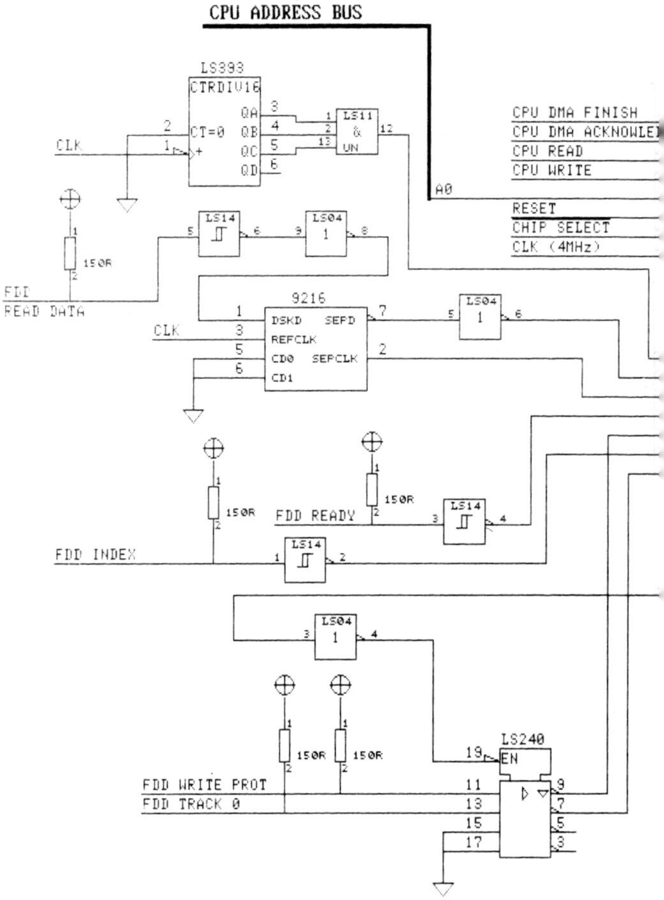

Figure 10.13 Circuit demonstrating the use of an 8272 FDC

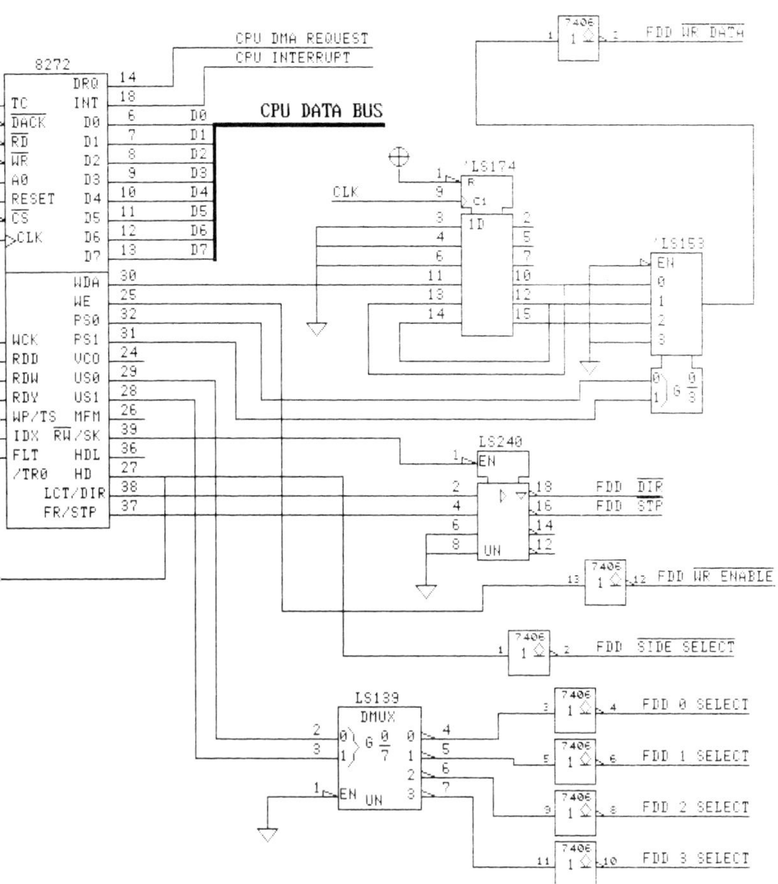

8272
CPU DMA REQUEST
CPU INTERRUPT
CPU DATA BUS
'LS174
CLK
'LS153
LS240
LS139
DMUX
7406
FDD WR DATA
FDD DIR
FDD STP
FDD WR ENABLE
FDD SIDE SELECT
FDD 0 SELECT
FDD 1 SELECT
FDD 2 SELECT
FDD 3 SELECT

11 Microprocessor Support Devices

11.1 INTRODUCTION

There are many ICs which may be used with microprocessors. These devices allow microprocessors to interface to the outside world. Intel, Motorola and Zilog produce a lot of microprocessor support devices and most of these are second sourced (produced by another manufacturer) which keeps the cost of the IC down. Most microprocessor manufacturers produce support chips for their micros. This chapter deals with a selection of the available support devices.

11.2 INTEL SUPPORT DEVICES

The data sheets for the following components may be found in Intel's Microprocessor and Peripheral Handbook and NEC's Microcomputers data book. The components to be discussed are listed below in Table 11.1, along with their approximate 1985 prices.

Intel number	*Description*	*Cost*
8202	Dynamic RAM Controller	£18.00
8203	64K Dynamic RAM Controller	£30.00
8231	Arithmetic Processing Unit	Not widely available
8251	Programmable Communication Interface	£2.50
8253	Programmable Interval Timer	£3.00
8255	Programmable Peripheral Interface	£2.50
8271	Programmable Floppy Disk Controller	£40.00
8272	Single/Double Density Floppy Disk Controller	£30.00
8275	Programmable CRT Controller	£25.00

Table 11.1 Intel Support Devices with approximate 1985 prices

11.2.1 8202 Dynamic RAM Controller

This device is very similar to the 8203, described in Chapter 6, except that it can only control dynamic RAMs with up to a 16K address space, i.e. 16Kx1, 16Kx8, 4Kx1, etc.

11.2.2 8203 64K Dynamic RAM Controller

This device is described in Chapter 6.

11.2.3 8231 Arithmetic Processing Unit

This device performs fixed and floating point arithmetic and trigonometric operations with 32 bit accuracy. It may be used to enhance the mathematical capability of a microprocessor system.

All transfers (operand, result, status and command) take place over an 8 bit bidirectional data bus.

The maximum clock frequency is 4MHz.

Some typical command execution times are given in Table 11.2.

Command	*No. of clock cycles*
Floating Point Addition	56–350
Floating Point Multiplication	168
SIN ×	4468
COS ×	4118
LN ×	4478
EXP ×	4616
ATAN ×	6006

Table 11.2 Typical command execution times for 8231

The 8231 may be used in a microprocessor based system to perform complex mathematical operations, which would take a long time for a program to execute.

11.2.4 8251 Programmable Communication Interface

This device is a Universal Synchronous/Asynchronous Receiver/Transmitter (USART). It may be programmed by the CPU to operate using virtually any serial data transmission technique. The USART accepts data characters from the CPU in parallel form and converts them into a continuous serial stream for transmission. Similarly it accepts serial data and converts it to parallel data. The USART signals the CPU when it wants to send or receive parallel data.

The synchronous baud rate is up to 64 Kbaud.

The asynchronous baud rate is up to 19.2 Kbaud.

The 8251 may be used as a serial port, which will allow the microprocessor system to be connected to a printer, or another computer, etc.

11.2.5 8253 Programmable Interval Timer

This is a programmable counter/timer which is arranged as three independent 16 bit counters, each with a count rate of up to 2 MHz. There are six modes of counting (all under software control):

Mode 0 (Interrupt on terminal count)
The terminal count is loaded into the selected count register. When the count reaches the terminal count then the output will go high, indicating that the count has finished. This can be used to program an exact delay, a timeout facility, etc.

Mode 1 (Programmable One Shot)
The output will go low on the rising edge of the gate input and the count will be started. At the terminal count, the output will go high.

Mode 2 (Divide by N counter)
The output will be low for one period of the input clock. The period from one output pulse to the next equals the number of input counts in the count register. This can be used as a pulse generator.

Mode 3 (Square wave rate generator)
The output will be high for one half of the count and low for the other half of the count. When the terminal count is reached, the counter is reloaded and the process is repeated. This can be used as a clock generator for, say, a printer. Different printers work at different baud rates. The output of an 8253 could be used to generate any baud rate required, simply by programming it.

Mode 4 (Software triggered strobe)
When the count is loaded, the counter starts. When the terminal count is reached, the output will go low for one input clock period and will then go high again. A possible use for this would be a software controlled timeout facility, i.e. if a message is sent by the μP and a reply is not received within one second, then some routine will be executed (perhaps via an interrupt).

Mode 5 (Hardware triggered strobe)
The counter will start counting after the rising edge of the trigger input and will go low for one clock period when the terminal count is reached. This can be used in a similar fashion to Mode 4.

11.2.6 8255 Programmable Peripheral Interface

This is a general purpose programmable I/O device. It has 24 I/O pins which may be individually programmed in two groups of 12 and used in three modes of operation.

Mode 0 Each group of 12 I/O pins may be programmed in groups of 4 to be input or output.

Mode 1 Each group of 12 I/O pins may be programmed in groups of 8 to be input or output. Of the remaining four pins, three are used for handshaking and interrupt control signals.

Mode 2 Eight lines are used as a bidirectional bus and five lines, borrowing one from the other group, for handshaking.

The 8255 has many uses, including being a parallel printer interface. Parallel printers accept data 8 bits at a time and hence are much faster than serial printers. Other uses for the 8255 include hard disk interfaces.

11.2.7 8271 Programmable Floppy Disk Controller (FDC)

This device interfaces one to four floppy disk drives to a μP. The 8271 FDC is compatible with the IBM 3740 soft sectored format, which is used by most microcomputers on the market. The 8271 is similar to, but less powerful than, the 8272, which is described in Chapter 10 (Memories).

11.2.8 8272 Single/Double Density Floppy Disk Controller

This is described in Chapter 10 (Memories).

11.2.9 8275 Programmable CRT Controller (CRTC)

This is a device which interfaces CRT raster scan displays to a microprocessor. (Monitors advertised in magazines, are raster scan.) Its main function is to refresh the display by buffering the information from main memory and keeping track of the display position of the screen.

The 8275 can be programmed to generate between 1 and 80 characters per row and between 1 and 64 rows per screen. It may, in conjunction with external circuitry, produce graphics on a CRT.

11.3 MOTOROLA SUPPORT DEVICES

The data sheets for the following components may be obtained from Motorola's Microprocessor Data Manual (8 bit) and Hitachi's 8 and 16 bit Microcomputer data book.

The components to be discussed are listed below in Table 11.3, along with their approximate 1985 prices:

Motorola number	*Description*	*Cost*
6821	Peripheral Interface Adaptor	£1.00
6829	Memory Management Unit	£40.00
6840	Programmable Timer Module	£3.50
6843	Floppy Disk Controller	£12.00
6844	Direct Memory Access Controller	£10.00
6845	CRT Controller	£6.50
6850	Asynchronous Communications Interface Adaptor	£1.10
6852	Synchronous Serial Data Adaptor	£2.50

Table 11.3 Motorola support devices with 1985 prices

Note: Motorola devices often have MC or MCM before the number.

11.3.1 6821 Peripheral Interface Adaptor (PIA)

This is a programmable I/O device which is similar to Intel's 8255. It has 20 I/O pins which are arranged in two groups of 8 I/O lines and 4 control lines. Each individual I/O line may be programmed to be either input or output. The 4 control lines are arranged in pairs corresponding to each group of 8 I/O lines.

Port A of the 6821 can drive CMOS logic directly (as well as TTL) and hence requires more drive current in the input mode than does port B.

11.3.2 6829 Memory Management Unit (MMU)

This device expands the addressing capability of a microprocessor (it was designed especially for the 6809) from 64 Kbytes to a maximum of 2 Mbytes. This expansion is accomplished by using a high-speed mapping RAM which is addressed by address bits A11–A15 and by a 5 bit task register. Each task is assigned memory in increments of 2 Kbytes up to a total of 64 Kbytes. Up to 8 MMUs can be used in a system and each MMU can handle four separate tasks. Hence a system with 8 MMUs, each handling four tasks of 64 Kbytes, has a 2 Mbyte address range.

11.3.3 6840 Programmable Timer Module

This is a programmable counter/timer, similar to Intel's 8253, which is arranged as three independent 16 bit counters. The count rates can be up to 4 MHz for the MC6840, 6 MHz for the MC68A40 and 8 MHz for the MC68B40.

11.3.4 6843 Floppy Disk Controller (FDC)

This device can control more than one floppy disk drive with external multiplexing. It is compatible with IBM 3740 format.

11.3.5 6844 Direct Memory Access Controller (DMAC)

This device transfers data directly between memory and peripheral devices by controlling the μP busses. The functional configuration of the DMAC is programmed via the data bus. There are four independent DMA channels in the 6844. There are three modes of transfer which involve single byte or block transfer. The maximum data transfer rate is 2 Mbyte/second.

11.3.6 6845 CRT Controller (CRTC)

This is a device similar to Intel's 8275. It provides video timing and refresh memory addressing. Alphanumeric, semigraphic and full graphic capabilities are available. The alphanumeric screen format may be defined by internal registers and an external timing source. Up to 512K of memory may be used in graphics mode—this gives 2048×2048 dot resolution for 8 bit wide memory (4096×4096 for 32 bit wide memory, etc.).

11.3.7 6850 Asynchronous Communications Interface Adaptor (ACIA)

The ACIA provides the data formatting and control to interface serial asynchronous data communication devices (such as a modem) to μPs. The communication with the μP is over an 8 bit bus.

The functional configuration of the ACIA may be programmed by the μP. The control register can be programmed to produce variable word lengths, etc. There are also three control lines which enable the ACIA to interface directly to a modem.

The maximum transmission rate is 1 Mbaud.

11.3.8 6852 Synchronous Serial Data Adaptor (SSDA)

The SSDA provides a bidirectional serial interface for synchronous data. The communication with the μP is over an 8 bit data bus.

The functional configuration of the SSDA may be programmed by the μP. The control registers can be programmed to produce variable word lengths, etc.

The maximum transmission rate is 1.5 Mbaud.

Typical applications for the SSDA include cassette controllers and floppy disk controllers.

11.4 ZILOG SUPPORT DEVICES

The data sheets for the following components may be found in Zilog's Components data book and Mostek's Microelectronics data book.

The components to be discussed are listed below in Table 11.4, along with their approximate 1985 prices:

Zilog number		*Description*	*Cost*
Z80 PIO	(Z8420)	Parallel I/O Interface	£2.50
Z80 CTC	(Z8430)	Counter/Timer Circuit	£2.50
Z80 DMA	(Z8410)	Direct Memory Access Controller	£7.00
Z80 DART	(Z8470)	Dual Asynchronous Receiver/Transmitter	£5.00
Z80 SIO	(Z8440)	Serial I/O Controller	£10.00

Table 11.4 Zilog Support Devices with approximate 1985 prices

Most of these devices are available in Z80, Z80A and Z80B versions.

11.4.1 Z80 PIO Parallel I/O Interface

The Z80 PIO is a programmable, two port device which provides an interface between peripherals and a μP.

All data transfer is done under interrupt control. The PIO can be programmed to interrupt the CPU on receipt of specified status conditions in the peripheral.

Each port may operate in one of 3 modes (4 in the case of port A):

Mode 1: Byte output
Mode 2: Byte input
Mode 3: Bit control
Mode 4: Byte bidirectional (port A only)

11.4.2 Z80 CTC Counter/Timer Circuit

The Z80 CTC is similar to Intel's 8253 and Motorola's 6840. It has four independent channels, although only three of them have external outputs.

11.4.3 Z80 DMA Direct Memory Access Controller

The Z80 DMA transfers data directly between memory and peripheral devices by controlling the μP busses. There are three basic functions:

1. Transfer of data between two devices
2. Search for a particular 8 bit maskable byte at a particular point in memory or I/O
3. Combined (1) and (2).

The Z80 DMA can interrupt the CPU on the successful termination of a search.

11.4.4 Z80 DART Dual Asynchronous Receiver/Transmitter

The Z80 DART has two channels and interfaces to serial asynchronous operation. The DART is merely a Z80 SIO which does not work with synchronous operation.

11.4.5 Z80 SIO Serial I/O Controller

The Z80 SIO has two channels and supports all common asynchronous and synchronous protocols, bit and byte oriented. It performs all of the functions usually done by UARTs and USARTs. There are separate control and status lines for modems or similar devices.

The maximum data rate is 800 Kbaud with a 4 MHz clock.

11.5 CONCLUSION

There are many other microprocessor support devices—this chapter only shows some of the more common ones.

Usually the support devices work best with their own μP, i.e. the Zilog devices work best with the Z80, the Intel devices work best with the 8080 and 8085, etc. However, it is not too difficult to mix and match, so to speak.

The data sheets for the devices mentioned in this chapter may be obtained from the relevant manufacturers or from data books.

12
Some Useful MSI ICs

12.1 Introduction

This chapter briefly explains the operation of several TTL devices which are commonly used in design and have not yet been discussed. The ICs to be discussed are listed below:

'05	Hex inverter with open collector outputs
'85	4 bit comparator
'138	3–8 decoder
'157	Quad 2–1 multiplexer
'174	Hex D type flip flops
'245	Octal Bus Transceiver
'367	Non Inverting tristate hex buffer
'373	Octal transparent latch
'670	4×4 register file.

Each of these components is available in 74, 74LS, 74S, etc.

12.2 '05 HEX INVERTER WITH O/C OUTPUTS

The circuit symbol for the 7405 is shown in Figure 12.1.

The pinout of the 7405 is the same as for the 7404—the only difference between the two is that the 7404 has totem pole outputs and the 7405 has open collector outputs.

The 7405 has many uses. For instance, wired OR configurations (discussed in Chapter 5—Analog Components) use open collector gates. A TTL signal can be converted to open collector simply by passing it through a 7405 (remember that the 7405 inverts the signal also).

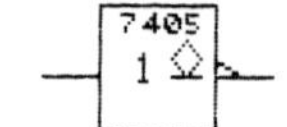

Figure 12.1 Circuit symbol for 7405

12.3 '85 4 BIT COMPARATOR

The circuit symbol for the 74LS85 is shown in Figure 12.2 and its function table is shown in Table 12.1.

The 74LS85 performs a direct comparison of two 4 bit binary numbers.

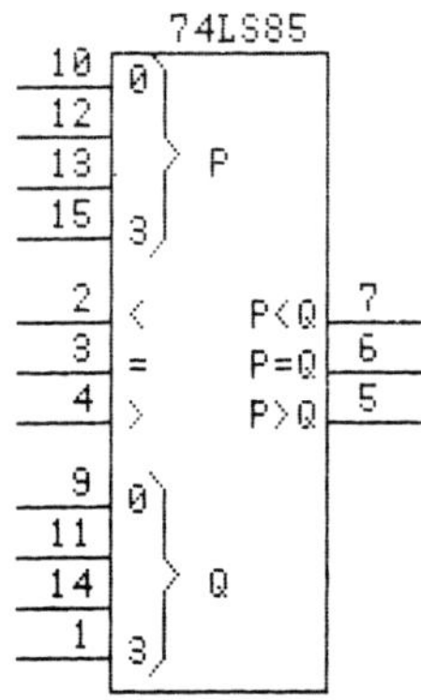

Figure 12.2 Circuit symbol for 74LS85

COMPARING INPUTS				*CASCADING INPUTS*			*OUTPUTS*		
P3,Q3	P2,Q2	P1,Q1	P0,Q0	P>Q	P<Q	P=Q	P>Q	P<Q	P=Q
P3>Q3	X	X	X	X	X	X	H	L	L
P3<Q3	X	X	X	X	X	X	L	H	L
P3=Q3	P2>Q2	X	X	X	X	X	H	L	L
P3=Q3	P2<Q2	X	X	X	X	X	L	H	L
P3=Q3	P2=Q2	P1>Q1	X	X	X	X	H	L	L
P3=Q3	P2=Q2	P1<Q1	X	X	X	X	L	H	L
P3=Q3	P2=Q2	P1=Q1	P0>Q0	X	X	X	H	L	L
P3=Q3	P2=Q2	P1=Q1	P0<Q0	X	X	X	L	H	L
P3=Q3	P2=Q2	P1=Q1	P0=Q0	H	L	L	H	L	L
P3=Q3	P2=Q2	P1=Q1	P0=Q0	L	H	L	L	H	L
P3=Q3	P2=Q2	P1=Q1	P0=Q0	X	X	H	L	L	H
P3=Q3	P2=Q2	P1=Q1	P0=Q0	H	H	L	L	L	L
P3=Q3	P2=Q2	P1=Q1	P0=Q0	L	L	L	H	H	L

Table 12.1 Function table for 74LS85

A possible use for the '85 is in a hardware "password" circuit. If you had an 8 bit password then, using two '85s, you could inhibit the operation of a circuit unless an entered value was equal to the password.

12.4 '138 3–8 Decoder

The circuit symbol for the 74S138 is shown in Figure 12.3 and its function table is shown in Table 12.2.

The 74S138 lowers one of its eight output lines in response to a particular code on its three input lines.

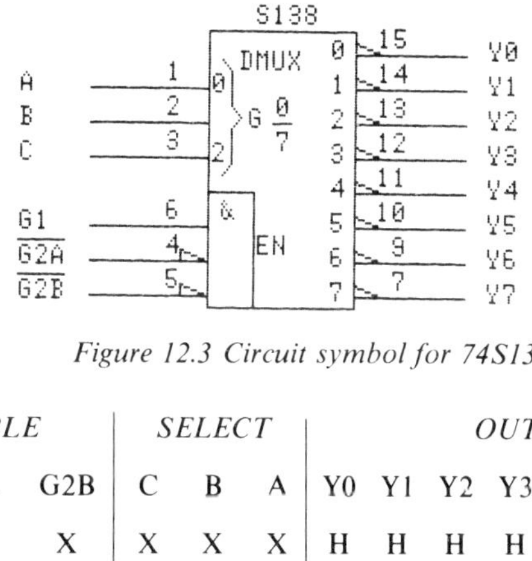

Figure 12.3 Circuit symbol for 74S138

ENABLE			*SELECT*			*OUTPUTS*							
G1	G2A	G2B	C	B	A	Y0	Y1	Y2	Y3	Y4	Y5	Y6	Y7
X	H	X	X	X	X	H	H	H	H	H	H	H	H
X	X	H	X	X	X	H	H	H	H	H	H	H	H
L	X	X	X	X	X	H	H	H	H	H	H	H	H
H	L	L	L	L	L	L	H	H	H	H	H	H	H
H	L	L	L	L	H	H	L	H	H	H	H	H	H
H	L	L	L	H	L	H	H	L	H	H	H	H	H
H	L	L	L	H	H	H	H	H	L	H	H	H	H
H	L	L	H	L	L	H	H	H	H	L	H	H	H
H	L	L	H	L	H	H	H	H	H	H	L	H	H
H	L	L	H	H	L	H	H	H	H	H	H	L	H
H	L	L	H	H	H	H	H	H	H	H	H	H	L

Table 12.2 Function table for 74S138

The '138 is very useful for address decoding with microprocessor based circuits. For instance, if A, B, and C inputs were connected to A13, A14, and A15 of, say, the Z80 bus and G1 was connected to

$\overline{RFSH}$ and G2A and B connected to $\overline{MREQ}$, then Y0 would be low for the range of memory addresses 0000H–1FFFH, Y1 would be low for the range 2000H–3FFFH, etc. Y0–Y7 are hence ideal for chip select signals. Most microprocessor systems have some sort of address decoding done in this manner.

12.5 '157 QUAD 2-1 MULTIPLEXER

The circuit symbol for the 74S157 is shown in Figure 12.4 and the function table is shown in Table 12.3.

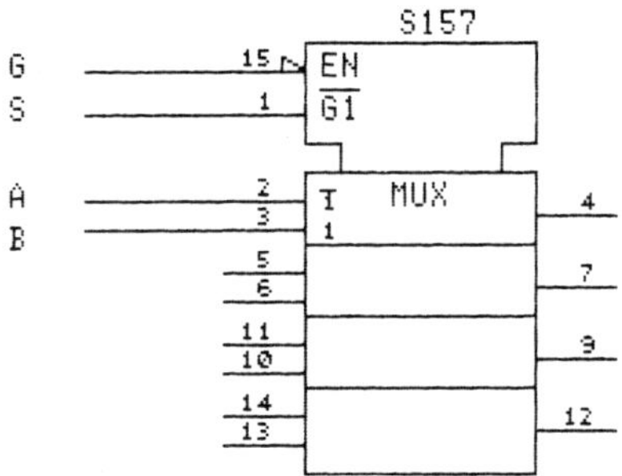

Figure 12.4 Circuit symbol for 74S157

INPUTS				*OUTPUT*
$\overline{G}$	S	A	B	Y
H	X	X	X	L
L	L	L	X	L
L	L	H	X	H
L	H	X	L	L
L	H	X	H	H

Table 12.3 Function table for 74S157

The '157 is useful for switching non tristateable inputs to a device. One of its uses is to multiplex addresses to a dual port RAM. A dual port RAM is an ordinary RAM which has circuitry around it which allows two devices to access it.

12.6 '174 HEX D TYPE FLIP FLOP

The circuit symbol for the 74LS174 is shown in Figure 12.5.

This device is useful if there are a lot of signals which need to be clocked by a common clock. For instance if you had five data lines which needed to be clocked into flip flops, then using 74LS74s you would need three 14 pin ICs. Only one 74LS174 is required to produce the same result. If individual Set, Reset and Clock lines were needed, then a 74LS74 would be more useful.

Another similar IC is the '273 Octal D type flip flop.

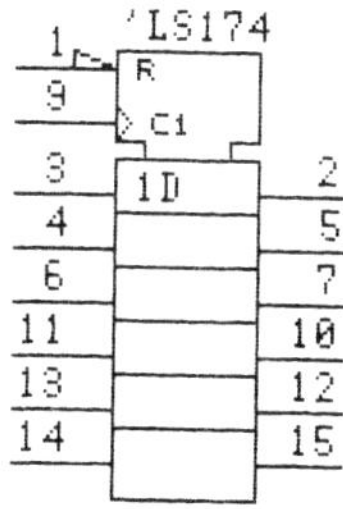

Figure 12.5 Circuit symbol for 74LS174

12.7 '245 OCTAL BUS TRANSCEIVER

The circuit symbol for the 74LS245 is shown in Figure 12.6 and the function table is shown in Table 12.4.

The 74LS245 is a tristateable bidirectional transparent latch.

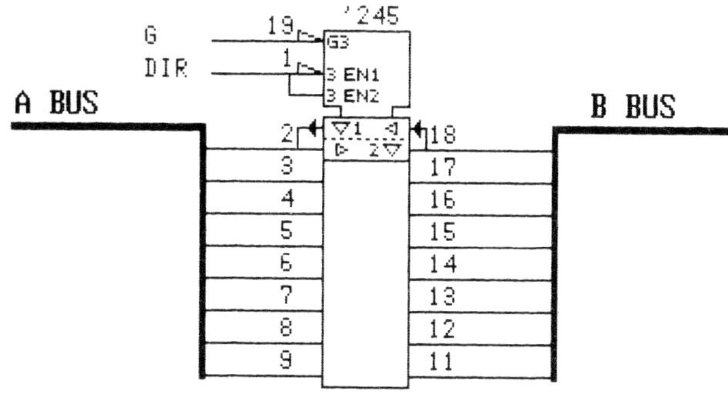

Figure 12.6 Circuit symbol for 74LS245

$\bar{G}$	*DIR*	*Operation*
L	L	B data to A bus
L	H	A data to B bus
H	X	Isolation (tristate)

Table 12.4 Function table for 74LS245

The '245 is useful for interfacing a bidirectional data bus with the data lines of, say, a dual port RAM. When the dual port RAM is talking to device A, then it must be isolated from device B. The '245 can do this easily.

This is demonstrated later in the chapter.

12.8 '367 NON INVERTING TRISTATE HEX BUFFER

The circuit symbol for the 74367 is shown in Figure 12.7.

When G1 is high, 1Q, 2Q, 3Q and 4Q are tristate.

When G2 is high, 5Q and 6Q are tristate.

When G1 is low, then 1D goes to the 1Q output, etc.

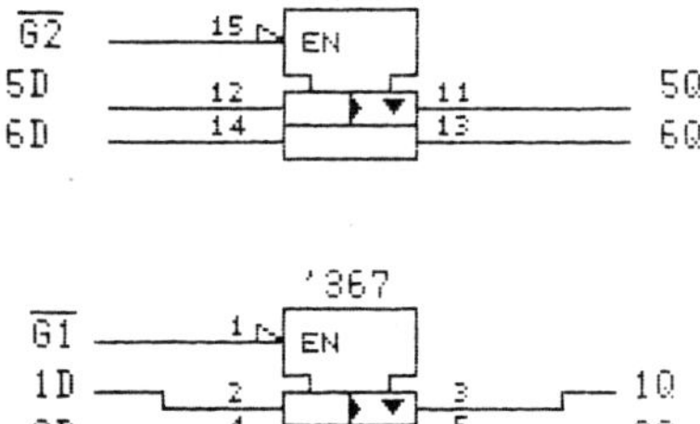

Figure 12.7 Circuit symbol for 74367

The '367 is a unidirectional version of the '245 and is used for similar purposes.

12.9 '373 OCTAL TRANSPARENT LATCH

The circuit symbol for the 74S373 is shown in Figure 12.8 and the function table is shown in Table 12.5.

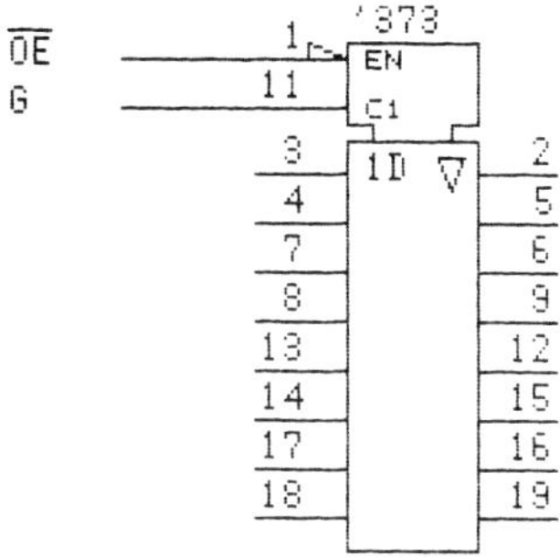

Figure 12.8 Circuit symbol for 74S373

$\overline{OE}$	*G*	*D*	*Q*
L	H	H	H
L	H	L	L
L	L	X	Q
H	X	X	Z

Table 12.5 Function table for 74S373

Note: Z indicates tristate.

The '373 is similar to the '367 except that the outputs may be "frozen" which can be very useful in many applications.

12.10 '670 4×4 REGISTER FILE

The circuit symbol for the 74LS670 is shown in Figure 12.9.

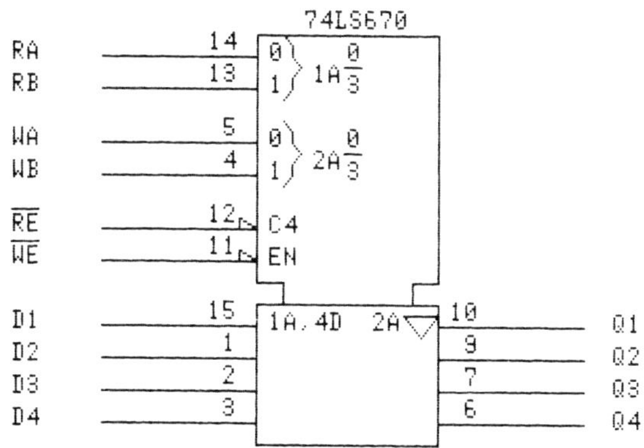

Figure 12.9 Circuit symbol for 74LS670

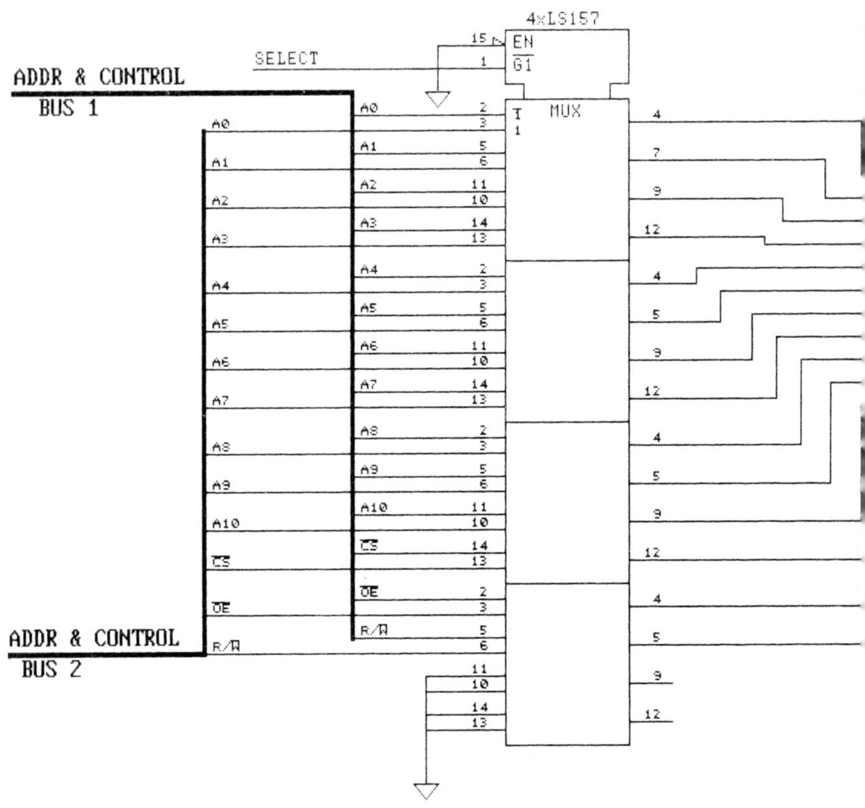

Figure 12.10 Dual port RAM

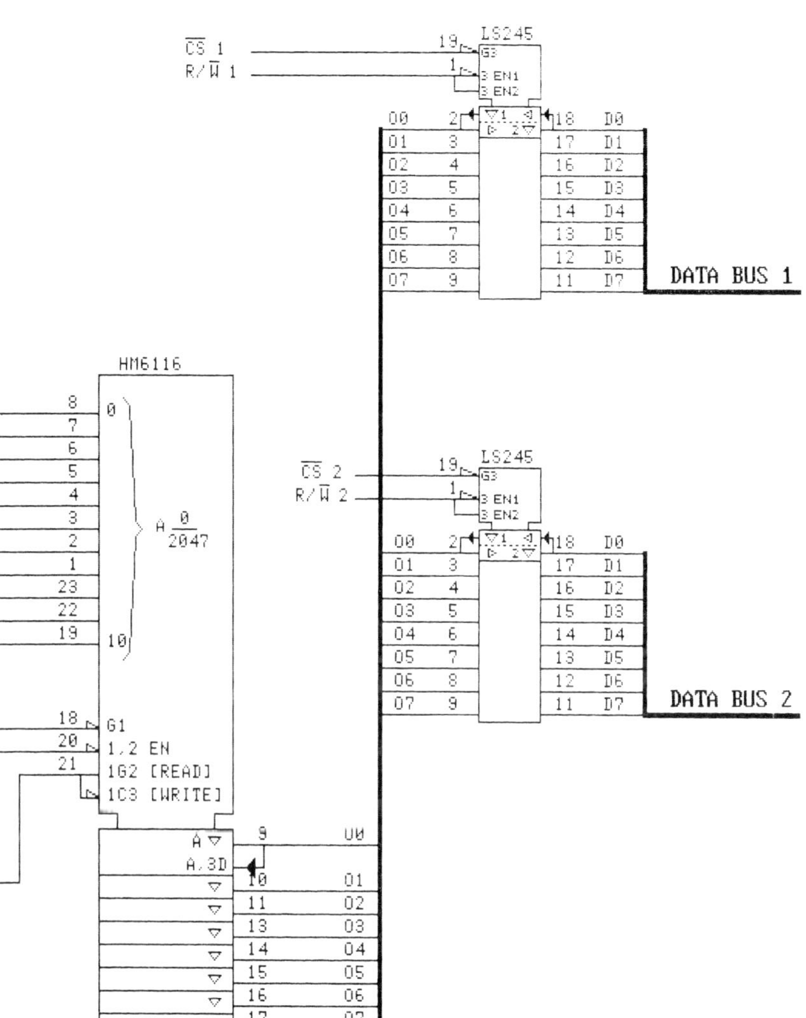
LS245
CS 1
R/W 1
DATA BUS 1
HM6116
A 0/2047
G1
1,2 EN
1G2 [READ]
1C3 [WRITE]
LS245
CS 2
R/W 2
DATA BUS 2

The 74LS670 allows simultaneous reading and writing to its registers. The access time for the 74LS670 is very fast. Since the read operation and write operations are independent, the 74LS670 may be used for communication between two devices which are not in synchronism (e.g. two microprocessors).

D1–D3	are the data inputs
RA,RB	is the address of the read data
Q1–Q4	are the data outputs
WA,WB	is the address of the write data
$\overline{WE}$	is the write enable
$\overline{RE}$	is the read enable.

The '670 is a dual port RAM device. It is very useful in that it does not require any external circuitry to implement the dual port function. Since it is so small, it cannot be used for major data transfer easily. However it is ideal for passing information between two devices completely out of synchronism with each other, e.g. two microprocessors.

12.11 EXAMPLE OF DUAL PORT RAM

Figure 12.10 shows a dual port RAM configuration, which uses some of the devices mentioned in this chapter.

The enables, etc. have to be signals which avoid contention (i.e. processor A trying to access the RAM at the same time as processor B). There are many ways to avoid contention. These are not discussed in this book.

12.12 CONCLUSION

This chapter adds to the design repertoire of the reader. The reader is advised to try designing simple circuits based around these devices.

13 Advanced LSI Components

13.1 INTRODUCTION

This chapter looks at two fields, normally left out of most discussions about digital design: Bit Slice logic and Custom ICs.

Most people regard bit slice logic with some trepidation, wrongly so because using bit slice logic is no different to using any other digital device.

Custom ICs are devices which the designer can define him or herself —these are rapidly gaining in popularity. Custom ICs may be LSI or VLSI, depending on their size.

13.2 BIT SLICE LOGIC

Bit slice logic consists of CPU building blocks. These blocks are LSI devices which may be configurated in different ways. This allows a custom CPU to be designed which has a unique set of microinstructions and macroinstructions. These macroinstructions may be as simple as Move Data from Register 1 to Register 2 or as complicated as multiply two 64 bit numbers together and store the decimal result in memory. One macroinstruction would suffice for both instructions. The great advantage of defining your own micro- and macroinstructions is that complex operations may be executed many times faster than if they were performed using a standard microprocessor (e.g. Z80). In addition, any size CPU may be produced. The largest μPs in 1985 have 32 bit internal data busses. Using bit slice logic, an 128 bit bus (or larger) may be used (this would use a lot of ICs). Another advantage of bit slice logic is that it may be used to emulate almost any computer. The two disadvantages of bit slice logic are the price (a Z80 costs approximately £3 and a bit slice CPU costs £20 upwards) and the

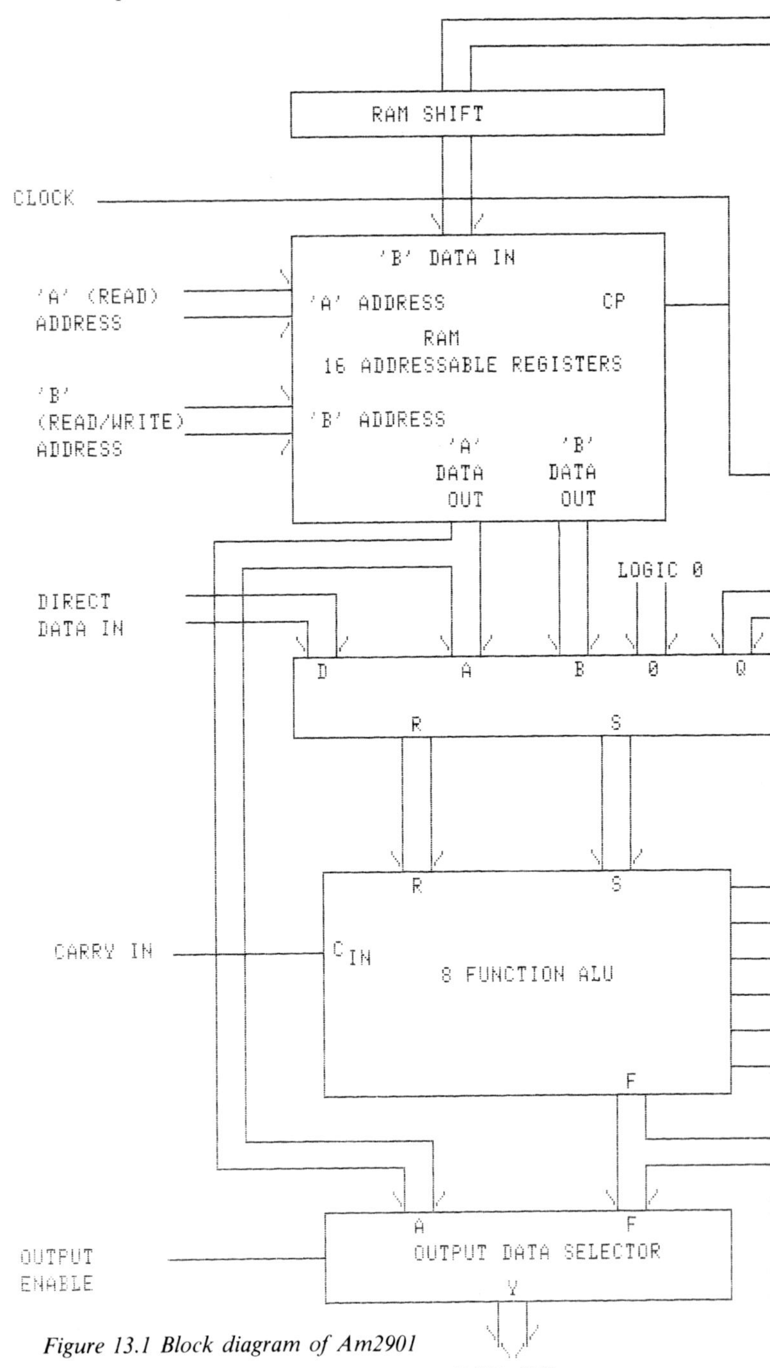

Figure 13.1 Block diagram of Am2901

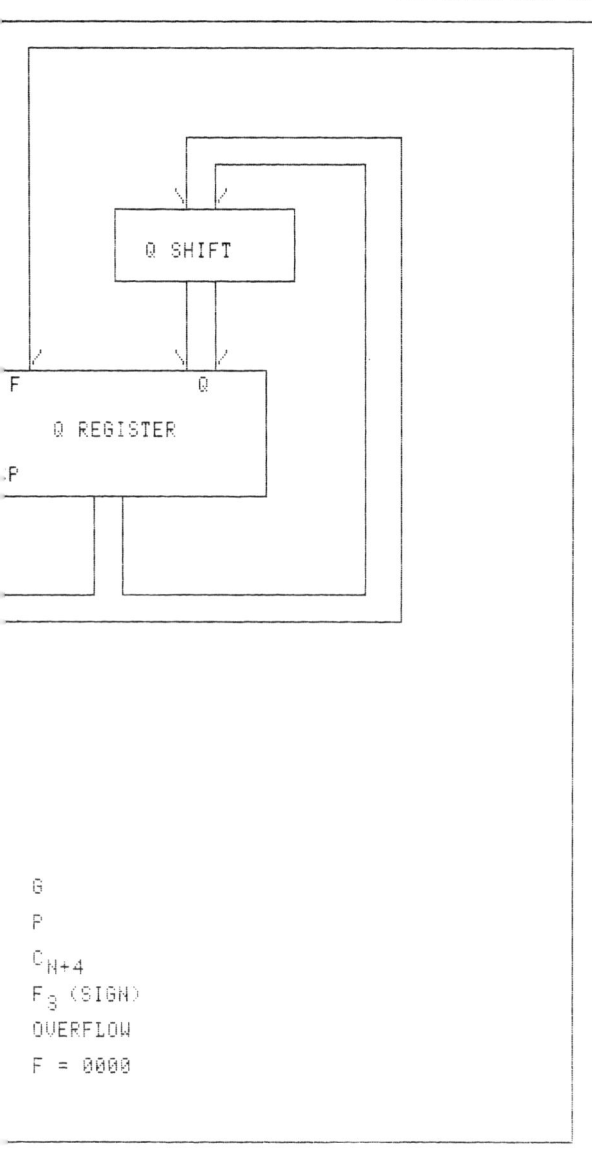
Q SHIFT
F
Q
Q REGISTER
P
G
P
C_{N+4}
F_3 (SIGN)
OVERFLOW
F = 0000

number of ICs required to make a bit slice CPU (over 10).

AMD produce the 2900 series, which are bit slice products. The 2900 series is second sourced by several manufacturers—some devices have 74 series equivalents. This section looks at some of the important ICs in the series. These ICs are listed below:

Am2901 4 Bit Bipolar Microprocessor Slice
Am2902 Look Ahead Carry Generator
Am2904 Status and Shift Control Unit
Am2909 Microprogram Sequencer
Am2914 Vectored Priority Interrupt Controller
Am2925 Clock Generator and Microcycle Length Controller
Am2930 Program Control Unit
Am2942 Programmable Timer/Counter/DMA Address Generator

The data sheet for these devices may be found in AMD's Bipolar Logic and Interface Data Book.

13.2.2 Am2901 4 bit bipolar microprocessor slice

The main features of the Am2901 are:

16 4 bit registers
2 independent access routes to the registers
8 function ALU
Shift operations
4 status flags
17 bit microinstruction input
Expandable to any number of bits.

The block diagram of the Am2901 is shown in Figure 13.1.

The register block may be accessed by 2 separate ports—A and B. Port A can only read data from the registers, while port B can read or write. The data out bits from each port goes into a multiplexer which drives the inputs of the ALU. The ALU has two 4 bit inputs. The multiplexer comprises one 2–1 multiplexer (port A data out and direct data in) and one 3–1 multiplexer (port B data out, shift output and zero). The output of the ALU goes to 3 places:

1. Shift register which can shift the data one position left or right.
2. Port B data in.
3. 2–1 mux (along with port A data out) which drives the Data Out lines.

The ALU accepts a Carry In from previous 2901s in a chain and produces four status flags, Carry Generate (G) and Carry Propagate (P) for use with a look-ahead carry generator such as the Am2902.

The eight ALU functions are:

R+S
R−S
S−R
R OR S
R AND S
$\bar{R}$ AND S
R XOR S
R XNOR S

The Am2901 is a 40 pin device.

13.2.3 Am2902 Lookahead Carry Generator

This is a high-speed device which accepts up to four pairs of Carry Progagate and Carry Generate signals and a Carry Input. It produces Carry signals for four ALUs (e.g. 4 Am2901s). Hence one Am2902 can be used with four Am2901s to produce a 16 bit processor. Five Am2902s may be used with 16 Am2901s to produce a 64 bit processor, etc.

The Am2902 is a 16 pin device.

13.2.4 Am2904 Status and Shift Control Unit

This IC replaces most of the MSI logic which is needed around an ALU, such as the Am2901. The Am2904 has four functions:

1. Status register
2. Condition code multiplexer
3. Shift linkage multiplexer
4. Carry In control multiplexer.

Shift Register

The Am2904 has two four bit registers which can store the four status outputs of an ALU. These registers are the micro status register (μSR) and the machine status register (MSR).

The μSR may be loaded by:

a. the four status inputs under Instruction control,
b. the MSR under Instruction control,
c. each bit may be individually set/reset under Instruction control.

The MSR may be loaded by:

a. the four status inputs under Instruction control,
b. the μSR under Instruction control,
c. the four parallel I/O pins under Instruction control,
d. each bit may be individually set/reset under Instruction control,
e. the four bit-enable inputs.

These registers can communicate with the system data bus via the parallel I/O pins.

Condition Code Multiplexer

The Am2904 can perform 16 different operations with the status registers. The outputs of the operations go to a 16–1 multiplexer and may be read by the outside world.

Shift Linkage Multiplexer

The Am2904 can perform 32 different shift and rotate operations using four I/O lines which connect to the ALU.

Carry In Control Multiplexer

The Am2904 generates the Carry Out from one of seven functions.

This is a 40 pin device.

13.2.5 Am2909 Microprogram Sequencer

The Am2909 is a 4 bit address controller which can sequence through a series of microinstructions in PROM or RAM. Several Am2909s may be cascaded to give any number of bits. The Am2909 can select an address from one of four sources:

1. Direct inputs

2. Direct register inputs (stored in an internal register)
3. 4 level push-pop stack
4. Program counter register (usually contains last address + 1).

The 4 level stack allows subroutines to be executed. This allows complex microprograms to be developed, using a minimum amount of PROM.

This is a 20 pin device.

13.2.6 Am2914 Vectored Priority Interrupt Controller

The Am2914 accepts 8 levels of interrupts, each of which may be individually masked. An 8–3 coder produces a 3 bit vector which corresponds to the highest level of unmasked interrupt. The Am2914 has a status register which contains the lowest priority that it will accept. After a vector is read from the Am2914, the status register is loaded with the vector. If an interrupt occurs which is of an equal or higher level than the value stored in the status register, then the Am2914 will produce an Interrupt Request.

The Am2914 is controlled by a 4 bit instruction field.

This is a 40 pin device.

13.2.7 Am2925 Clock Generator and Microcycle Length Controller

The Am2925 produces eight combinations of four different clock waveforms. The Am2925 may run at over 31 MHz. Run/Halt and Single Step controls are provided.

This is a 24 pin device.

13.2.8 Am2930 Program Control Unit

The Am2930 is a 4 bit Program Control Unit which does for macroinstructions what the Am2909 does for microinstructions. Several Am2930s may be cascaded to give any number of bits.

The Am2930 can select an address from four sources:

1. Direct Inputs

2. Register Inputs
3. 17 level Push-pop stack
4. Program Counter register.

The Am2930 has 32 instructions, 16 of which depend on the Condition code input (usually a direct connection from the Am2904).

The instruction set is split into five types:

1. Unconditional fetch
2. Conditional jump
3. Conditional jump to subroutine
4. Conditional return from subroutine
5. Miscellaneous.

This is a 28 pin device.

13.2.9 Am2942 Programmable Timer/Counter/DMA Address Generator

The Am2942 is an 8 bit device and may be cascaded with other Am2942s to produce any number of bits.

The Am2942 may be used as a Programmable Timer/Counter or a DMA Address Generator.

The Am2942 has 16 instructions, eight for each function.

When used as a counter/timer, the Am2942 provides two independent 8 bit up-down counters. These two counters may be connected to produce a single 16 bit counter.

When used as a DMA Address Generator, the Am2942 provides sequential memory addresses for sequential data transfer to and from a memory. It has a word count and provides a DONE signal when the transfer is complete.

This is a 22 pin device.

13.3 CUSTOM ICs

There are two types of custom ICs—Full Custom and Semi-Custom. Full Custom ICs allow more complex circuitry than Semi-Custom, but are much more difficult and expensive to design.

13.3.1 Semi-Custom ICs

There are two major types of Semi-Custom ICs. These are the gate array and cellular design. Gate array ICs have an array of simple gates laid out in the chip. Computer programs can be used to interconnect these gates to produce more complex devices. The advantages of gate arrays are that they have a low design cost and a fast turnaround time (design to production). The disadvantages of gate arrays are that a lot of space is wasted by unused gates and the power consumption is high.

Cellular design is based on a set of standard functions (e.g. 74LS174 equivalent), called cells, which have all of the details required for production already stored. All that the engineer needs to do is to connect these cells together to implement his design. The advantages of cellular design over gate arrays are that there is less wasted space, the speed of operation is increased, and the power consumption is lower.

Cellular designs tend to be more expensive than gate arrays in very small quantities ($<$100), but they are cheaper for medium sized quantities.

13.3.2 Designing Using Semi-Custom

To design a gate array IC, an engineer would take a proven (in TTL) design along to a company that dealt with gate array designs. This company would have a computer with a library of standard functions which contained the interconnections required to make more complex devices (e.g. flip flop). The engineer would redesign his circuit in terms of these standard functions, many of which will be similar to standard TTL functions. After he has redesigned his circuit and input the circuit connections to the computer, the computer will run a test program to test all of the logic using either test data input by the engineer or its own test data (self generated). When running this test program, the computer will work out approximate connection lengths to use for propagation delays. The test program will check timing constraints as well as functional constraints (whether the circuit has the correct functionality). Once the engineer is satisfied with the test results, the circuit is "laid out" by another program which works out exactly where every connection will go. The test program is now run again, with exact connection lengths. If the circuit passes this test, then the engineer will have a good degree of confidence in the IC and it will go to silicon (be produced).

Cellular based designs are very similar in approach.

13.3.3 Full Custom ICs

Full Custom design involves defining the exact layout of the silicon, metalization, etc. in the IC. Hence this is a very lengthy and complicated job. The advantages of full custom over semi-custom are that the power consumption is lower, the speed of operation is greater, and the silicon efficiency is higher (hardly any wasted space). The disadvantages are the very high design cost and the difficulties in designing from scratch (although there are some CAD programs to aid designers). However, for very large quantities, full custom ICs are much cheaper than for an equivalent complexity using semi-custom.

13.4 CONCLUSION

This chapter rounds off the new devices introduced in this book.

Bit Slice logic can be very useful for high speed, high technology designs, as can custom ICs. Both of these fields are fascinating and the reader is advised to study them in further detail.

14 The Project Life Cycle

14.1 INTRODUCTION

This chapter describes the various stages within a project, going from the initial specification to the Post Design Service.

A big company will often contract work out to a small company. This is usually done if the big company already has too much work for its resources, or if the work needs to be completed in a hurry (small companies have less inertia than most large ones). The work may take the form of a computer, a terminal, a part of a larger system, a peripheral, etc. The life cycle of such a project is as follows:

1. Specification of the design.
2. Planning.
3. Production of circuit diagrams, timing diagrams, etc.
4. Production of first prototype.
5. Production of PCBs.
6. Post Design Services.

14.2 SPECIFICATION

This is split into two parts:

1. The vendor (big company) gives the contractor (small company) a product specification. This should include:

a. Full functional details of how the product must operate.
b. Full interface details (how it connects to the outside world).
c. Dimensions and appearance of the product.
d. Environmental details of the product.
e. Timescales.
f. Any other constraints (e.g. agency approval).

a. Full functional details

This may be brief or lengthy. It must contain sufficient information for the contractor to produce the product that the vendor desires. Often this is incomplete because the vendor does not really know exactly what he or she wants.

b. Full interface details

This is often included in (a) and must give baud rates and other details for printer and other interfaces.

c. Dimensions and appearance

This describes what the product must look like and what must be its size.

d. Environmental conditions

This gives ranges of operating conditions under which the product must work. These details include temperature, humidity, shock, electrostatic discharge, etc.

e. Timescales

This gives dates by which various things must be done (e.g. first prototype, completion of circuit diagrams, etc.). These usually have monetary penalties attached to them for late delivery.

f. Any other constraints

There are various agencies who test new products for things like Electromagnetic Interference (EMI) emission, which can cause radio waves which produce interference on aeroplanes, etc., safety factors, etc. Many governments now only allow products to be sold to the public if they have agency approval:

In Europe, VDE is the main agency.
In USA, UL and FCC are the main agencies.
In Canada, CSA is the main agency.

2. After the contractor has received the vendor's specification, he or she makes sure that he or she understands everything that is in that specification. Anything which is totally unclear can usually be explained in a telex message or a telephone call. (Incidentally, keep copies of *all* correspondence with anyone, especially outside your company.) It is very unusual for a vendor's specification to be completely watertight—there are usually some ambiguous points. Hence the contractor now produces his or her own design specification, based on the vendor's specification. The vendor's specification can be thought of as "This is what we would like you to do" and the contractor's specification can be thought of as "This is what we are going to do". At this point the vendor and the contractor get together and discuss the two specifications, eventually coming up with a definitive specification which forms the basis of a contract between the vendor and the contractor. This contract will include the contractor' price—the normal method of payment is one-third at the start of the project, one-third on demonstration of a fully working prototype and one-third on completion of the product. There will be "milestones" in the project—dates by which various parts of the project must be completed. There are usually penalty clauses in the contract associated with these milestones.

14.3 PLANNING

No project can be sensibly started without planning. The planning function is to work out how long each stage in the project will take and how many people are required. For instance if a particular project had two PCBs, both independent, each of which would take 20 man weeks (1 man working for 20×5 days), then the project would take 40 man weeks. If there were two men on the project, it would take 20 weeks. Depending on the number of people in the company (resources) and the number of projects going on, one of these two options would be more desirable. It may be best to have one man for 30 weeks and two men for 5 weeks, etc. Planning will show which is the best route to follow.

Planning is never completely accurate—there are always external factors (e.g. people off sick, etc.), but it is a very good approximate guide. After someone has done several projects, then he will have a "feel" for how long a similar project will take. This, of course, comes with experience.

Throughout a project, the plans are continuously updated to reflect any deviations from the original plan. This allows management to put more resources on a project that is slipping (getting behind schedule). Progress meetings, once a fortnight or once a month, can be used to update the plans for all of the projects which a company is involved in. There are several graphical methods of showing the progress of a project (PERT charts, etc.). These and other details about planning can be found in most books on the subject.

The initial plans for the project will be drawn up before the contract is signed.

14.4 DESIGN OF THE CIRCUIT

As part of the production of the design specification, some initial design will be done. This is known as the feasibility stage. Once the contract has been signed, the design starts in earnest. Usually the hardware is designed by one person, the software by other people, and one person looks after the project. In a project which involves several PCBs, one person usually looks after each PCB. In this sort of project, the exact interface between each PCB must be worked out, as well as which functions of the circuit will be implemented in hardware and which in software.

The hardware/software interface is very important. The project leader and the hardware and software engineers will discuss exactly how the design will be implemented.

After the various interfaces have been worked out, each engineer goes off to design his or her part of the project. The hardware engineer will produce circuit diagrams, along with timing diagrams to check them. He or she will also produce a description of the circuit, which will help someone else to comprehend the circuit diagrams.

The engineer will keep a log book of items concerned with the project. *This is a very important thing to do.* The log book will include all decisions pertaining to the hardware, including informal discussions, telephone conversations, etc. It is very useful to be able to pick up a log book six months after an event and have a ready answer to a question. Remember that the designer is responsible for his or her design even after it is completed.

When the engineer is happy that his or her design will work, then a design review will take place. This involves another hardware engineer, usually someone unassociated with the project, sitting down with the circuit diagrams, timing diagrams, circuit description, and any other relevant information. The second engineer will go over the design in detail, making sure that the design is sensible and pointing out any errors. It is very important to have someone, other than the designer, doing this—the designer will find it very difficult to spot his or her own mistakes. When the second engineer is satisfied with the design then the circuit can be built.

14.5 PRODUCTION OF FIRST PROTOTYPE

If time is of the essence, and the engineer is very confident in the design, then the circuit may go straight to PCB without building a prototype. This can cut down the project cycle by 4–6 weeks but can prove costly in time and money if the circuit needs too many modifications. Usually one prototype is built first. There are several ways of getting this done—solder wrap, wire wrap, speedwire, etc. Of these I favour solder wrap, which involves soldering the wire to each pin, thus ensuring a good contact. The problem with all of these methods is that it is very easy to break a wire or even make wrong connections.

Once the prototype has been built, it is a good idea to "buzz it out" against the circuit diagram (check that each connection is made). This is a tedious job, but does give confidence that the circuit has been built correctly. Other checks to make are whether 0V and +5V are connected together; if all of the ICs are positioned correctly (all in the same orientation); etc.

After these initial checks have been completed, the circuit is ready to be debugged. Very seldom does a circuit work 100 per cent first time, even the simple ones. The first thing to do is to switch on, without any of the expensive ICs in position, and ensure that the power supply is supplying the correct voltages to the circuit. After that you should check that the outputs of the expensive ICs are not being driven by any other device (use an oscilloscope) and that the power connections are correct. Once you are sure that no expensive IC will be blown up, switch off the power, insert the remaining ICs and switch the power on again. This, again, is slightly tedious, but it can save time and money. The same sort of thing should be done with any device which is expensive or fragile (e.g. monitors and floppy disk drives).

When the basic tests have been finished, the circuit can be tested. There is a large range of test equipment available, much of which can be rented.

After the circuit has been debugged, the software engineer will want to have the prototype to test the software. The hardware and software engineers then work together to fully test the system functionally (hardware and software). Once they are happy that the system works as it should, liaising with other engineers and the project leader, then a design review meeting is held. This meeting should include the engineers who did the design, the project leader, someone from Quality Assurance (QA), someone from Manufacturing and another engineer (the chairman of the meeting), preferably of the same status as the project leader. All of the updated documentation (circuit diagrams, timing diagrams, etc.) will be distributed before the meeting so that everyone has a chance to read them. At the meeting, the engineers who did the design will be asked questions on their design by QA, Manufacturing, and the chairman. The idea of this meeting is to ensure that the circuit has been fully tested and that design rules have been adhered to.

When the design review board are satisfied with the prototype, then the vendor is shown the prototype and will, hopefully, approve it and hand over the second installment of the money. The prototype can now go to PCB.

14.6 PRODUCTION OF PCBs

This is split into two parts—CAD and PCB manufacturing. The CAD (Computer Aided Design) will take the circuit diagrams, parts list, and layout constraints, and will produce photography for a PCB manufacturer to make PCBs. The layout constraints include the following information concerning the PCB:

Exact dimensions of the PCB
Exact positions of all mounting holes
Special positioning of parts of the circuit
Design rules (e.g. all ICs must have the same orientation)
Any lettering on the PCB (e.g. © Ben Bourdillon).

This package of information is taken to a CAD company, who will produce a net list (containing all the connections in the circuit). The engineer will check this net list against the circuit diagrams and tell the CAD company of any errors. Once the engineer is satisfied with the net list, then the CAD company produce a proposed layout, which shows the position of every component on the PCB. A penplot is done of this layout and this is sent to the engineer to be checked. The engineer should check this penplot very carefully because it is easy to make changes now, but not later. Things to look for are analog circuitry (which should be close together), whether the layout constraints have been followed (it does not always happen), etc. The project leader will also check the penplots to spot anything that one person might have missed.

After the penplots have been checked, the CAD company starts routing the connections on the PCB. Again, they should be following the designer's layout constraints. Once all of the routing has been done, the engineer will get penplots of the routing. These need to be checked carefully for violation of layout constraints and any other errors, which may be the fault of the CAD company, or may be the fault of the engineer. The project leader should also check these.

When the final penplots have been authorized, the CAD company produces a set of photoplots for the PCB manufacturer. These photoplots are:

Side 1 (solder side) copper
Side 2 (component side) copper
Side 1 solder mask
Side 2 solder mask
Side 1 silk screen (optional)
Side 2 silk screen
Drill master or drill tape.

The copper and solder mask define where the tracks go on the PCB, and the silk screen has lettering on it (IC numbers, etc.) to aid manufacturing and testing of the PCB. The drill master contains all the holes in the PCB. This may be produced on a magnetic tape for a PCB drilling machine.

The above photoplots are for a double-sided PCB. There are single-sided PCBs and multilayer PCBs which may have as many as 16 layers at present. With 16 layers, there will be 16 copper photoplot and 16 solder masks, but obviously still only one or two silk screens and one drill master.

These photoplots should be checked as a final guarantee that the PCB will be correct. Once they have been checked, they will be sent to a PCB manufacturer who will produce copies of them, manufacture the PCBs from the copies and send the master photoplots and PCBs back. The PCBs can then be tested as for the prototype. It is a good idea to put sockets in the first PCB to be tested in case any ICs are blown up (it is difficult to unsolder an IC from a PCB without damaging the PCB). In addition, one PCB should be left unpopulated (bare board) so that tracks which are obscured on the PCB under test can be easily traced.

At this point, any case being produced for the product can be tested for size.

Again, it is very seldom that the first PCB is the final one, since it is impossible to remember everything to tell the CAD company, that CAD company will probably make mistakes, and the design may even have changed while the PCB was in CAD. Hence two or three iterations of the PCB may be necessary. Each time the CAD company can take the PCB in its previous form and alter it slightly (if the changes are not too major). This reduces the cost and time and increases the accuracy of the finished product.

The approximate CAD times are 1 week to net list
1 week to layout penplots
3 weeks to final penplots
2 days to photoplots

PCB production can be between 1 day and 20 days for small quantities.

14.7 POST DESIGN SERVICES

After the vendor is satisfied with the product, he or she will hand over the final third of the money in return for a working PCB, the photoplots, the parts list, the circuit diagrams and any other relevant documentation. However that is not the end of the story. The contractor is morally and contractually obliged to correct any design errors found during the vendor's testing or at any other time. Hence if, in two years time, the vendor comes back and says that there is a timing problem when they use a particular brand of IC for IC27 then it is up to the contractor to check if there really is a problem and, if there is, to find a cheap and efficient remedy. This is where log books are really useful—especially if a decision concerning that part of the circuit is documented in the log book.

14.8 CONCLUSION

This chapter should give the reader an idea of how a project works.

Not all companies will run projects in this manner—some have much more bureaucracy (most large companies fall into this category) and some have much less (usually very small companies without design experience).

Appendices

APPENDIX A DECIMAL, BINARY AND HEXADECIMAL CONVERSION TABLES

Decimal	*Binary*	*Hexadecimal*
0	0000	0
1	0001	1
2	0010	2
3	0011	3
4	0100	4
5	0101	5
6	0110	6
7	0111	7
8	1000	8
9	1001	9
10	1010	A
11	1011	B
12	1100	C
13	1101	D
14	1110	E
15	1111	F
16	1 0000	10
17	1 0001	11
18	1 0010	12
31	1 1111	1F
32	10 0000	20
255	1111 1111	FF
256	1 0000 0000	100
4095	1111 1111 1111	FFF
65535	1111 1111 1111 1111	FFFF

APPENDIX B RULES OF BOOLEAN ALGEBRA

1.	Commutative laws	$A+B=B+A$ $A.B=B.A$
2.	Associative laws	$A+(B+C)=(A+B)+C$ $A.(B.C)=(A.B).C$
3.	Distributive law	$A.(B+C)=A.B+A.C$
4.	DeMorgan's Theorems	$\overline{A+B}=\overline{A}.\overline{B}$ $\overline{A.B}=\overline{A}+\overline{B}$
5.	General	$A+0=A$ $A.0=0$ $A+1=1$ $A.1=A$ $A+A=A$ $A.A=A$ $A+\overline{A}=1$ $A.\overline{A}=0$

APPENDIX C HOW TO MAKE A D TYPE FLIP FLOP FROM BASIC GATES

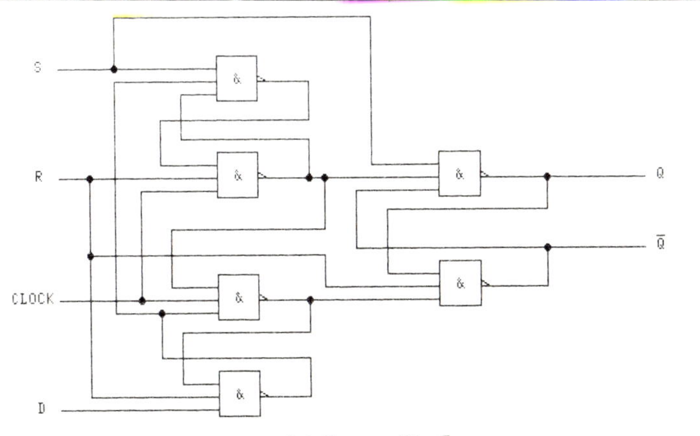

Figure C.1 D type flip flop

APPENDIX D RATIONALE BEHIND THE NEW SYMBOLS

1. Introduction

The conventional set of symbols, used in circuit diagrams, do not show how inputs affect the outputs. To find out how inputs affect outputs, it is necessary to look at the internal logic. The International Electrotechnical Commission has developed a symbolic language that shows the relationship of each input to each output. This system uses dependency notation.

2. General rules

a. Input lines go into the left-hand side of a symbol, output lines come out of the right-hand side. If there is an exception to this, an arrow will indicate direction.
b. Common input lines go into a common control block, as shown in Figure D.1.
c. The internal logic 1 state corresponds to an active signal (this is true for positive and negative logic).

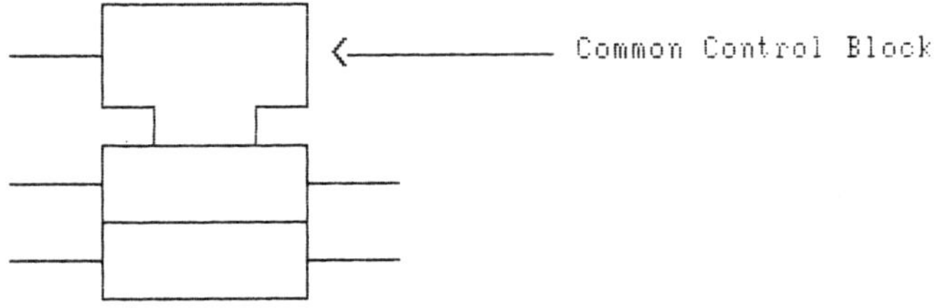

Figure D.1 Common Control Block

3. Symbols inside and outside the outline

This section shows some of the symbols that may be found inside and outside the outline:

Active low input (an external 0 produces a 1 internally).

Active low output (an internal 1 produces a 0 externally).

Signal flow from right to left.

Bidirectional signal flow.

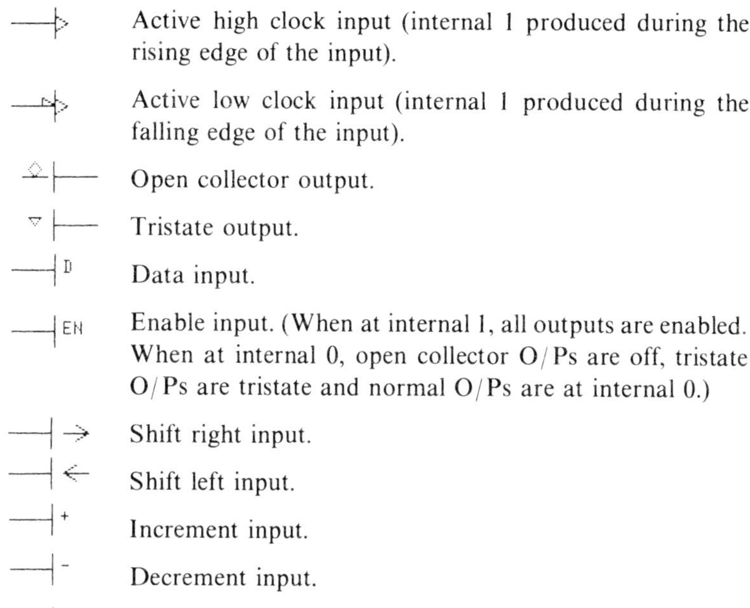

Figure D.2 Symbols inside and outside the outline

4. Dependency notation

Some of the rules of dependency notation are:

a. The input or output which affects other inputs or outputs must be labelled with a letter, representing the relationship, and an appropriate identifying number.

b. The inputs and outputs affected by that input or output must be labelled with the same number.

c. If an input or output is affected by more than one other input or output, then the numbers of the affecting inputs or outputs will be separated by commas in the label of the affected input or output.

There are ten basic types of dependency letters. These are:

G AND
V OR

N XOR
Z Interconnection
C Control
S Set
R Reset
EN Enable
M Mode
A Address

The first four of these are shown in Figure D.3.

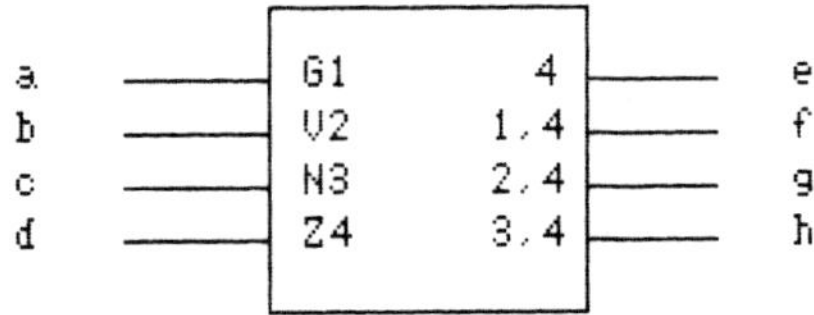

Figure D.3 Example to show AND, OR, XOR and Dependency

In Figure D.3, the e output will be the same as the d input.
the f output will be affected by the a input, etc.

Hence, effectively:

$e = d$
$f = a.d$
$g = b+d$
$h = c \oplus d$

Control is shown in Figure D.4.

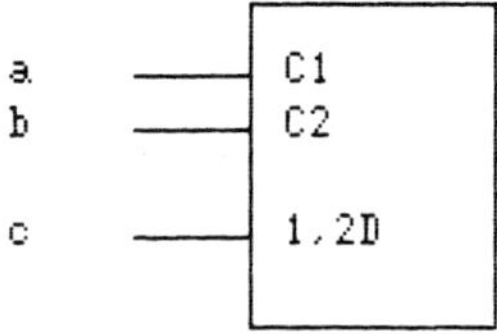

Figure D.4 Example to show control

The data on c will be latched if both a and b are active.

Set and Reset are used as for flip flops.

Enable has been previously explained.

Mode is shown in Figure D.5.

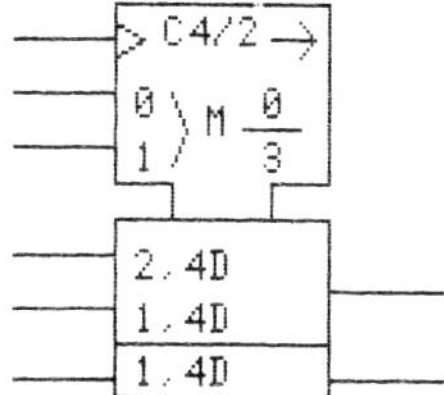

Figure D.5 Example to show Mode

In mode 0 and 3, no change occurs.
In mode 1, if a clock comes in on a, then e and f will be latched.
In mode 2, if a clock comes in on a, then the data will be shifted right and data will be input from d.

Address is shown in Figure D.6.

When e is active, the data on f is latched into one of eight locations, defined by b, c, and d.

When a is active, then g will output the data stored at the location defined by b, c, and d.

APPENDIX E STANDARD RESISTOR AND CAPACITOR VALUES

Resistor values		*Capacitor values*	
1.0×10^x	$(x = 0$ to $6)$	1.0×10^x	$(x = -12$ to $0)$
1.2×10^x		1.5×10^x	
1.5×10^x		1.8×10^x	
1.8×10^x		2.2×10^x	
2.2×10^x		3.3×10^x	
2.7×10^x		4.7×10^x	
3.3×10^x		6.8×10^x	
3.9×10^x		8.0×10^x	
4.7×10^x			
5.6×10^x			
6.8×10^x			
8.2×10^x			

Hence typical resistor values are 1K8, 4K7, 220R, 33R, 1M2, etc.;
typical capacitor values are 220pF, 4.7nF, 0.1μF, etc.

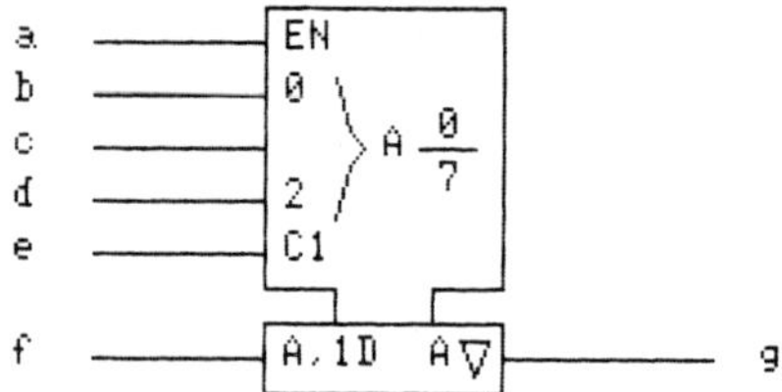

Figure D.6 Example to show address

APPENDIX F CLOCK GENERATOR CIRCUIT

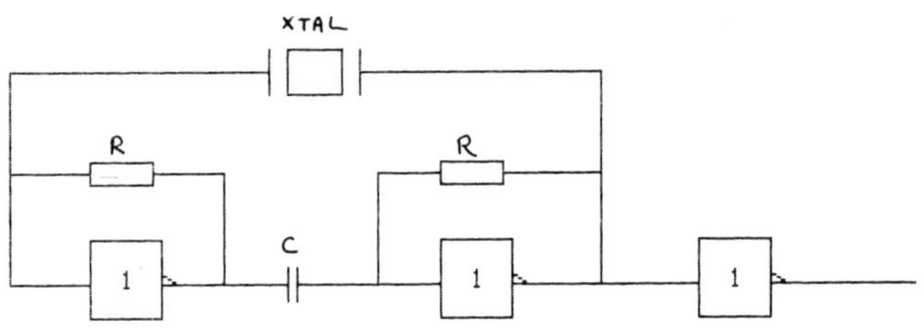

Figure F.1 Clock circuit

This circuit is based on two NOT gates, each with feedback via a resistor. The resistors are used to bias the NOT gates so that they are on the verge of switching from high to low or vice versa. The crystal regulates the speed at which the NOT gates are allowed to switch and hence determines the frequency of the output signal. The capacitor is used to filter out any unwanted high frequency signals.

The third NOT gate is used to isolate the clock driver circuit from the rest of the circuit.

Different types of NOT gate ('04, 'LS04, 'S04, etc.) have different bias voltages and so different values of resistors need to be used.

APPENDIX G FUNCTIONAL INDEX/SELECTION GUIDE

This appendix gives a list of some useful devices, in various categories:

74 SERIES TTL

NAND gates

Hex Inverters	'04
Quad 2 input NAND	'00
Triple 3 input NAND	'10
Dual 4 input NAND	'20
8 input NAND	'30

NOR gates

Quad 2 input NOR	'02
Triple 3 input NOR	'27
Dual 4 input NOR	'25
Dual 5 input NOR	'260

AND gates

Quad 2 input AND	'08
Triple 3 input AND	'11
Dual 4 input AND	'21

OR gates

Quad 2 input OR	'32

XOR gates

Quad 2 input XOR	'86

Arithmetic

1 bit full adder	'80
2 bit full adder	'82
4 bit full adder	'83
4 bit ALU	'181, '381
Look ahead Carry Generator	'182
4×4 multiplier	'284, '285, '274

Tristate buffers

Octal transceivers	'245
Non inverting hex buffers	'365, '367
Inverting hex buffers	'366, '368

Non inverting quad transceivers	'243
Inverting quad transceivers	'242

Flip flops and latches

Dual D type	'74
Dual J–K edge/pulse triggered	'73, '76, '109
Quad D type	'175
Quad J–K	'276
Hex D type	'174
Octal D type—2 state	'273
Octal D type—3 state	'374
Octal transparent latch	'373

Shift registers

8 bit PIPO	'299
4 bit PIPO	'195
8 bit SIPO	'164
8 bit PISO	'165, '166
8 bit SISO	'91

PLAs

16 input, 8 output fixed OR	'PL16L8
16 input, 8 registered output fixed OR	'PL16R8
14×32×6	'PL839

Counters

4 bit synchronous binary	'161, '163
Synchronous decade	'160, '162
4 bit asynchronous binary	'93, '293
Asynchronous decade	'90, '290

Multiplexers/Demultiplexers

8–1	'151
Dual 4–1	'153, '253
Quad 2–1	'157, '257
3–8	'138
Dual 2–4	'139

Bipolar memories

512×8 PROM	TBP28S42
32×8 PROM	TBP18SO30
32×8 RAM	'218
4×4 register file	'670

Other devices

Microprocessors

Intel 8 bit	8048, 8748, 8080, 8085, 8088
Zilog 8 bit	Z80
Motorola 8 bit	6800, 6809, 68008
Mostek 8 bit	6502
Intel 16 bit	8086, 80186, 80286
Zilog 16 bit	Z8001, Z8002
Motorola 16 bit	68000
Motorola 32 bit	68020

Microprocessor Support Devices

DMA controllers	Intel 8237 and 8257, Zilog Z80 DMA, Motorola 6844.
APUs	Intel 8231 and 8232.
Counter/Timers	Intel 8253, Zilog Z80 CTC, Motorola 6840.
Floppy disk controllers	Intel 8271 and 8272, Motorola 6843.
CRT controllers	Intel 8275, Motorola 6845, Mostek 6545.
Peripheral I/Fs	Intel 8255, Motorola 6821.
UARTs	Intel 8251, Zilog Z80 SIO and PIO, Motorola 6850.
Dynamic RAM controllers	Intel 8202 and 8203, AMD Am2964.

Index